The Beams of Our House

A Biblical Framework for a Christian Home

*"The beams of our house are cedar,
and our rafters of fir."*
Song of Solomon 1:17

The Beams of Our House

Dr. Wayne Hudson

All scripture references used in this book are from The King
James Version.

Cover Design by
Linda K. Holton/Faith Baptist Church Publications
Edited by Cheryl Suarez

Printed in the USA by
Faith Baptist Church Publications
Fort Pierce, FL 34982
www.fbcpublications.com

ISBN 978-1-888237-46-5

To order more copies of *The Beams of Our House*, contact:

Dr. Wayne Hudson
Phone: 940-337-9572
www.JustPreachingJesus.com

To Harvey and Beatrice Hudson, my parents,
who gave me an example
of what a Christian home should be.

And to my devoted wife Susie Harred Hudson,
my helpmeet for forty years, and who is
irreplaceable in a lifetime of building
a Christian home together.

Table of Contents

Acknowledgements

To Ben Burdick and Cheryl Suarez, without whose talents and persistence this manuscript would still be gathering dust in my office.

To Paula Roberts and Tira Schulz for their technical assistance and encouraging comments, which brought fresh excitement for what the Lord may do through this book.

To the congregation and staff of Bayou Drive Baptist Church, for whom this book was first written and by whose support it is now published.

Foreword

It is amazing how man will search for another theory to better present his argument. We all have seen this done in many areas. You can find a theory on most any problem that plagues man. I find that no matter how many theories go astray, man will still trust that one will be found to correct his problems.

This is particularly true in the area of the home. Volume after volume they write, with their own understanding, never giving thought to the only book ever written that has the answers for the home and everyone included in the home. That book is the Word of God. It holds no theories, only truth.

My dear friend and Christian brother, Pastor Wayne Hudson, has written this truthful book on the subject of the home. Not one theory will you find when you read this excellent book that deals with every aspect of the home. From the book of Genesis through the books of the New Testament, God has given man His will for happiness in the home. Every husband and father, wife and mother, and children of all ages will find God's will in His Word.

Bro. Wayne Hudson has for many years been a diligent student of the Word. It has been his guide in his ministry as a pastor and teacher. The truth, not another theory, makes up the contents of this most excellent presentation on the Christian home. Any member of the family who desires a better understanding of the Christian home will profit greatly by making a thorough study of Brother Hudson's presentation. Clearly he has presented the position of the father, mother and children in a truthful, scriptural presentation. I highly recommend it to all who desire to know the truth concerning the Christian home.

    Evangelist C.L. Roach
    Powder Springs, Georgia

The author and his credibility as well as the writing itself determine the value of any book. I am pleased to commend both.

I have been acquainted with Dr. Wayne Hudson and his family for many years. Wayne Hudson has a great Christian heritage. His great-grandfather was an old-time circuit-riding Baptist preacher. His grandfather, though not a preacher, was godly and known in his community as a man of prayer. His father, Harvey Hudson, was a wonderful, compassionate, Bible preacher also given to prayer.

Dr. Hudson is married to a gracious Christian lady, Susie, who for these forty-one years has been and still is his most staunch supporter. The Hudsons have two sons, Kevin and Brantley. Kevin and his family are members of Bayou Drive Baptist Church, where he serves as Associate Pastor with his father. Brantley and his wife are active workers in a Baptist church in Austin, Texas.

This treatise is not a "how to" book. It is deep, thought provoking, and soul searching, containing relevant information for those who want to honestly know God's plan concerning marriage and the home. This book contains great truths, backed by Bible principle and quotation, expressed in a plain and yet unique way; easily understood by all who sincerely seek to know spiritual truths concerning a godly marriage—the kind God intends for all; one that impacts today's world.

In my opinion, this volume is worthy of reading and re-reading, being filled with truths from God's Word to be obeyed. The couple that reads and practices the contents revealed herein will no doubt experience the blessings of God on their lives, marriage and family.

Pastor A. W. Cooper
Athens, Texas

What Has Happened to the Family?

"The beams of our house are cedar, and our rafters of fir." Song of Solomon 1:17

God has a plan for marriage and families. He set the family on course with the creation of Eve and with His instructions to Adam: *"Therefore shall a man leave his father and mother, and shall cleave unto his wife: and they shall be one flesh"* (Genesis 2:24). Since that time His plan has been carried out through the family. The Bible is full of examples of men and women who were less than perfect, but were able to be blessed and pleasing to God because they served Him through their families. Of course, there have always been those who rebelled, choosing to do their own will their own way. But God's blessing has always been on the family. Marriage and family were God's first and only plan. Yet they are still the most current of all of God's institutions, and the cornerstones of any society of civilized people. Both institutions are under attack today—an attack against the very things God designed to hold society together.

Our country was founded and built by families. Families overcame disease and deprivation to build the first community at Plymouth. Pioneer families pushed ever westward to successfully extend the United States of America. Farmers, industrialists, scientists and patriots, as families, became the backbone of America.

Primarily through those families, America became a God-fearing and God-blessed nation.

Families are truly different today than they were in the past. Two world wars changed the social structure of the country, causing families who had been isolated to be suddenly thrust into world economies and social pressures not known before. The post-war years of the forties and fifties set the stage for major changes in the family. The family has been under attack in the last forty-plus years as never before in our society. Even many Christians are casualties in this war on marriage and the family, and children of this generation are permanently scarred by the attack.

Whether we want to admit it or not, we are not traveling by horse and buggy today. Our society has changed—some oddly call it progress, but the truth is that the family has changed. At least one thing has not changed throughout the centuries—God's plan for the family and His provision to make it succeed. Answers for the family in this age will not be found by looking backward with sentimentality, but by looking into the pages of God's Word. There we will discover His plan for keeping marriage and families successful in the most anti-family age that the world has ever known.

The quotes that follow summarize the changes in the makeup of the family in recent times. American statistician George Barna says, "The made-for-TV Clever family (of the *Leave It to Beaver* series) provided a weekly portrayal of some of the realities facing the American family. Addressing those issues were the working father, the homemaker mother, and the two children under the age of eighteen who lived in that home." This makeup "represented 60 percent of American households in 1960. Today, that same configuration represents just 3 percent of all American households."[1]

The change in the family is illustrated by the words of Hillary Rodham Clinton in a commencement address delivered at George Washington University on May 8,

1994: "If it ever did, [the American family] no longer does consist of two parents, two children, a dog, a house with a white picket fence, and a station wagon on the driveway. Instead of families looking like the Cleavers on *Leave It to Beaver*, we have families that include test tube babies and surrogate moms....instead of aunts and uncles and grandmas and grandpas, we have nannies and day care centers."[2]

These statements are somewhat shocking. To say the least, we live in a changed society. Any change in society affects everyone in the society, including the family. Let's note these changes.

🌲 Many Styles of Families 🌲

Newsweek magazine, in a special edition dedicated to "The 21st Century Family," spoke of the diversity of families: "The American family does not exist. Rather, we are creating many American families, of diverse styles and shapes...we have fathers working while mothers keep house, fathers and mothers both working away from the home; single parents, second marriages bringing children together from unrelated backgrounds; childless couples; unmarried couples, with and without children; gay and lesbian parents."[3]

Marriage: Optional

"Three out of five couples who marry this year will live together for some period of time before tying the knot. That constitutes a fivefold increase in just the last two decades...Studies show that those who live together

---

1 *Family in America*, a national research study conducted by the Barna Research Group, February 1992, Quoted in *Home Improvement* by David Jeremiah.

2 Quoted in *Focus On the Family* Newsletter, p. 1, August 1994.

3 Jerrold Footlick, "What Happened to the Family," *Newsweek* special edition (winter/spring 1990) p. 15. Quoted in *Home Improvement* by David Jeremiah.

before marriage are 80% more likely to wind up getting divorced than are those who do not."[4]

"Hollywood has so glamorized cohabitation by unwed partners, even fathering children out of wedlock, that it has now taken on an aura of legitimacy in the eyes of most people."[5]

Same-sex Families

One of four adults now believes that there is nothing wrong with two people of the same sex getting married, and that those who do are a family.[5] This is a growing trend and is more widely accepted every day.

Single-parent families

"In 1990 our government estimated that 60% of children born in America that year would live in a single-parent home at some point before they turned eighteen years old...When these trends started a few decades ago, the experts predicted children would rebound and make it through without harm...We now know that the experts were wrong." Single parents try hard to give the extra amounts of love for their children. My hat is off to those who go the extra mile to provide financially, socially and spiritually for their children. But statistics show that the children will have increased developmental, learning, and emotional problems.[5]

Multi-layer families

The following quote describes the typical multi-layer family: "The original plot goes like this: 'First comes love, then comes marriage, then comes Mary with a baby carriage.' But now...John and Mary break up. John moves in with Sally and her two boys. Mary takes the baby Paul. A year later Mary meets Jack who is divorced

---

4 Data provided by the National Bureau of Economic Research.

5 David Jeremiah, *Home Improvement,* Turning Point for God, 2001.

with three children. They get married. Paul, barely two years old, has a mother, a father, a stepmother, a step-father, five stepbrothers and stepsisters—as well as four sets of grandparents, and countless aunts and uncles. And guess what? Mary's pregnant again."[6] Many multi-layer families are even more complicated.

Marriage Deferred

"In 1960 almost three-quarters of all adults twenty-five or older were married, but by the mid-90's less than half of that age group was married. The median age of a person's first marriage was twenty-one years of age in 1960; by the mid-90's it had jumped to twenty-five."[5]

Why is this? There are at least two reasons. It has become socially acceptable to enjoy all the benefits of marriage and family (e.g., sex, children, companionship) without making a commitment to the responsibilities that accompany them. Also, the mess that Americans have made of family life no doubt disgusts some young people and causes them to want no part of it.

Mothering Declining

Childbearing in the 1950's and 1960's was expected—almost a duty. Then came many repeated warnings about the dangers of over-population. Since then the size of the American family has declined. By the middle 1990's the average family had only 2.6 people.[5]

Material Motivation

"The 'stay at home mom' is a vanishing breed in America. In the decade of the 1990's more than two-thirds of all women were employed in the American work force."[5] Sadly, this statistic holds true even for those women with pre-school children.

---

6 Barbara Kantrowitz and Pat Wingert, "Step by Step," *Newsweek* (winter/spring 1990) 24. Quoted in *Home Improvement* by David Jeremiah.

Mushrooming Child-care

"We have grown from less than 150,000 children enrolled in child care in 1960 to more than 2 million in 1990...Families spent more than $14 billion on child-care in 1989."[7]

Divorce

"Since 1960 the rate of divorce has quadrupled... about one out of every four adults in the nation has experienced at least one divorce. Among those adults who divorce and remarry, the probability of going through another divorce is even higher; in excess of 60 % of all divorced adults who remarry will divorce again."[8] The disillusionment of divorce is traumatic. So many people now approach marriage with the idea of "giving it my best shot." But if trouble starts, they walk away with no real commitment to marriage. As a pastor, I have seen the heartache and tears that divorce brings. The evidence of the lasting scars upon families, our society, even on the church, is steadily increasing.

Are you disillusioned about the family by now? Well, take heart. Society may have changed its opinion of marriage and family, but God has not. The Biblical definition of family is still one man and one woman for one lifetime that will rear their children in the nurture and admonition of the Lord. Jesus voiced the unchanging mind of God when He said, *"Have ye not read, that he which made them at the beginning made them male and female, and said, For this cause shall a man leave father and mother, and shall cleave to his wife: and they twain shall be one flesh? Wherefore they are no more twain, but*

---

7 Monthly Labor Review, December 1989, 49. Quoted in *Home Improvement* by David Jeremiah.

8 George Barna, *"The Future of the American Family,"* Families, ed. *Jerry B. Jenkins (Chicago: Moody Press) 10-11.* Quoted in *Home Improvement* by David Jeremiah.

one flesh. What therefore God hath joined together, let not man put asunder" (Matthew 19:4-6).

🌲Timeless Truths for Uncertain Days 🌲

Having seen the attack upon the family and the chaos destroying it from within, how do you and I avoid the traps? How can we build a home that will be pleasing to the Lord? How can we be happy and successful in our marriages? How can we raise children that will be strong and faithful servants of Christ? Sometimes it seems that the chaos of the world around us is like a minefield, impossible to cross without great devastation, damage, and ruin.

If we honestly look at the situation of marriage and family in this day, we find the outlook very bleak, perhaps even hopeless in some cases. Sometimes the very foundations of society, marriage and family, seem rocked and broken beyond repair. But the Bible has the answers. Bible principles are the framework that is missing in most homes today. It is that framework, built on the solid Rock of the Lord Jesus Christ, which makes marriage and families strong. The answers are still to be found on the pages of God's Word. The never-changing Word of God contains promises and instructions so that we can be as strong and fruitful as God intended us to be. The promises become reality as we read, study, and obey His Word as it applies to our marriages and families. We can construct the framework, the lasting "Beams of Our House," as we follow His direction in the following areas, establishing and maintaining the Word of God in each.

🌲 Biblical Marriage Relationships 🌲

"The beams of our house are cedar, and our rafters of fir" (Song of Solomon 1:17).

Isn't it foolish to think that God would create a man

and a woman, give them the wonderful feeling we call romance, a mysterious institution like marriage, and the passion of sexual intimacy, then not have anything to say to them about it all? We sometimes approach the marriage relationship as if it is a magician's black box that we just kind of fiddle around with until we figure it out. That is just not God's way. He gives explicit instructions for all areas of our life pertaining to salvation, Godliness, holiness, fulfillment, and living above compromise. He also gives instruction for our marriage relationships.

The Song of Solomon has much to say about the relationship between a husband and wife. That relationship, when laid in Christ, is the foundation of the Christian home. Sometimes called "The Song of Songs on the Theme of Themes—Love," The Song of Solomon traces the development of the marriage relationship and details many of its aspects. The book runs the gamut of the relationship built between a young woman of lowly background and the prince she loves. The details of the relationship are all there, from the honeymoon to the first fight and reconciliation. The purity and exquisite delight of the relationship is such that is becomes the analogy divinely used to typify the relationship of Christ with His church. Surely we also need to examine and abide in the instruction of this "Manual for Marriage Relationships."

In Song of Solomon chapter one we have the beginnings of that relationship. There are parts of the interaction of the courtship that we are not informed about, as if we are missing the first act of a play. The romance is well under way in chapter one. Although we don't know all the details, we are given enough information to know that this couple has fallen pretty hard for each other. We are privileged to eavesdrop on a very private conversation between the two of them.

The conversation seems to be about building a home. Although the building is a future dream, the prince seems to say to the Shulamite, "The location or construction of the physical house doesn't really matter. If we will depend on Him and serve Him in faith, He will build a house for our shelter and safekeeping."

🌴 Biblical Marriage Responsibilities 🌴

"But Christ is all, and in all" (Colossians 3:11).

Biblical marriage responsibilities are not the physical responsibilities of making a living or keeping house, which we all have. The responsibilities that the Bible deals with are those of a husband and wife toward each other. These Bible principles must be in place for the marriage relationship to be right.

We see the progression from responsibility to relationship in capsule form in Colossians chapters three and four. These scriptures give instructions for every relationship that will be faced upon this earth: wives to husbands, husbands to wives, children to parents, fathers to children, servants (workers) to masters (bosses), masters to servants. Before any of these relationships are specified, the writer Paul describes what we are calling responsibilities. He lists them in the context of being assumed or "put on" by the "new man". Of course, none of these can be accomplished by the unbeliever, but only by the saved and growing Christian. (Remember that growing does not mean perfect.)

The first responsibility is that of making sure that *"Christ is all, and in all"* (Colossians 3:11). This verse does not refer to Christ's work in our salvation, but rather to His domination in every aspect of our lives—thought patterns, affections, ambitions, and plans. In other words, we must make Jesus Lord of all that we do. Certainly Christ should be all of our church life, but we must also make Him all of home life, business life, recreational life, and all other aspects of life. The attributes that follow are the natural outgrowth of letting Christ be all in all, and are impossible to attain if we refuse this one responsibility.

"Put on therefore, as the elect of God, holy and beloved, bowels of mercies, kindness, humbleness of mind, meekness, longsuffering; Forbearing one another, and forgiving one another, if any man have a quarrel against any: even as Christ forgave you, so also do ye. And let the peace of God rule in your hearts, to the which also ye are called in one body; and be ye thankful. Let the word of Christ dwell in you richly in all wisdom" (Colossians 3:13-16).

When Christ is all in all to us, we are to put on the attributes listed in the above scriptures: "mercies, kindness, humbleness, meekness, longsuffering, forbearance, and forgiveness" (verses 12-13). Can't you sense the relationship growing sweeter already? After listing these attributes, Paul greatly stresses the motivation of a Christian's actions—love (verse 14). Two more attributes are added in verse 15, "the peace of God" and thankfulness, then finally we are brought back to the Word of God in verse 16. Paul indicates that all these things will produce a joy and love toward the Lord, and that the grace of God will overflow our hearts. When this is true, everyone around us will be affected.

Every relationship will be right if responsibilities toward the Lord are right. When responsibilities toward the commands of Christ are right, the marriage relationship becomes the product, an overflow of the grace of God in our hearts.

When our responsibilities are aligned with these Biblical principles, our marriage relationships will be as God intended them to be. When we fail in these areas, we can expect to fail in our relationships, also. One thing we must remember is that these responsibilities are not something that we do once, then never have to do again. The responsibilities never go away. There is always an urgency to be motivated by love, to allow Christ to be all, to forgive, etc. We will succeed in our relationships as we submit ourselves to the responsibilities of God's Word everyday.

🌴 Principles for Blessings in the Christian Home 🌴

"And whatsoever ye do in word or deed, do all in the name of the Lord Jesus, giving thanks to God and the Father by him" (Colossians 3:17).

"And whatsoever ye do, do it heartily, as to the Lord, and not unto men" (Colossians 3:23).

Little children sing a song in Sunday school called "The B-I-B-L-E". One of the verses says,

"The B-I-B-L-E,
Yes, that's the Book for me.
I read and pray and then obey
The B-I-B-L-E."

Paul seems to have had the order of this song in mind when he penned Colossians 3:17, 23. There certainly is a time for reading and understanding Bible principles, and there are some things that we must pray over as we set priorities in our lives. But there also comes a time when reading and praying are past. At that point there must be obedience.

Our relationships are listed in Colossians 3:18-4:1, not with lengthy descriptions—most of them are only a sentence or so in length. But there is a common thread that runs through all of them—each relationship requires action. There is a pivotal verb in each instance: *"wives, submit;" "husbands, love;" "children, obey;" "fathers, provoke not;" "servants, obey;"* and *"masters, give."* Just knowing the Word of God is not enough. If we want the blessings of God in our homes, we will have to obey the Word of God in our homes. Obedience is an action word, and obeying usually requires moving away from the 'status quo'.

The very fact that you have read this far shows that you are interested in improving either your marriage relationship or marriage responsibilities, or you are looking for added blessings upon your home. Let me quickly say that none of these come automatically. It will require work on your part to put these principles into action (there's that word again). How many times have you inwardly agreed with God about something that you read in His Word, but have done nothing about it? How many books such as this one have you read, mentally consented to, and then filed away to be forgotten—accomplishing nothing?

Some people just go through the motions of a relationship. Others are very action-oriented—there's always something going on there. Some are somewhat sedentary and inclined toward little or no action. Still others are somewhat jaded, having tried all of it before, and are half-hearted in their actions. No matter what our past responses, we are motivated to action by the principles of Colossians 3:17, 23: every effort is done in the name of Jesus with an attitude of glorifying the Father; every effort is executed toward the Lord and not toward men.

Doing all in the name of Jesus becomes natural when we do our homework in the marriage responsibilities, and *"Christ is all, and in all."* Our efforts to build a relationship will continue, even when we have been wronged or hurt, because our motivation will be the love of Christ. This is the key to overcoming the selfish attitudes that are the root cause of failure in the home relationship.

Marriage and family are lifetime relationships, requiring long-term effort to maintain. Most of us start out willing to make some effort, but over time the storms come: finances, debilitating diseases, failures, rebellion of children, even death. In times of adversity, the only answer is to keep looking to the Lord and doing what we do with the understanding that it is as "unto the Lord". No situation or person can disrupt our relationship as long as our focus is on the Lord.

Many families today are distraught, even dysfunctional. These are perilous, frightening, and frustrating times for marriage and the family. Some might even say that marriage and family are out of date and doomed. But God is still concerned about the family and it is He who builds the house.

In the pages of this book we will investigate the beams of that house—the house the Lord builds—the foundation, the support walls, the joists, the rafters, and the roof that make up the Christian home. They are all there in the Word of God. The raw material is laid out. Each Christian has the tools for its construction: the Bible, prayer, discernment, and application. Our construction superintendent is the leadership of the Holy Spirit. God waits for each of us to put in place *"The Beams of Our House."*

Photo:

Mike and Brenda Herrmann were married at Bayou Drive Baptist Church, May 18, 1991. Mike is with the Lord; Brenda lives in New Braunfels, Texas, and is a godly single mom raising their son Michael.

Part One

Biblical Marriage Relationships

*Therefore shall a man
leave his father and his mother,
and shall cleave unto his wife.*
Genesis 2 :24

1

Marriage is a Divine Relationship

Marriage is not a scheme for cohabitation and child-bearing dreamed up by some psychologist or legislator. Marriage is the plan of God. God puts great priority on our marriage relationship.

🌲 A Relationship That Pleases God 🌲

"And the LORD God said, It is not good that the man should be alone; I will make him an help meet for him" (Genesis 2:18). Seven times in Genesis 1 God said His creation was good. In Genesis 1:31 God said that everything was very good — pleasing, desirable, and fitting. Now, in all of this perfect creation, one thing was not good. The thing that was not good in the eyes of God was that "the man should be alone." In other words, it was not pleasing, desirable, or fitting for man to be alone.

"Whoso findeth a wife findeth a good thing, and obtaineth favour of the LORD" (Proverbs 18:22). God says that it is good — pleasing, desirable, and fitting — for a man to have a wife. He also says that that man has found favor — the granting of grace from God.

"But and if thou marry, thou hast not sinned; and if a virgin marry, she hath not sinned. Nevertheless such shall have trouble in the flesh: but I spare you" (I Corinthians 7:28).

I include this verse for the phrase *trouble in the flesh.*
Paul says in the first part of the verse that there is no
sin in the marriage relationship itself. Then he says that
the flesh will have some problems with the relationship.
Once married, the spouses must fulfill each other's needs.
Marriage truly is a giving of self to the spouse. Our flesh
does not like this principle, but it is a Spiritual principle,
as we will see in a later lesson. (Remaining single can
also cause problems in the flesh. *"Nevertheless, to avoid
fornication, let every man have his own wife, and let
every woman have her own husband"* [I Corinthians 7:2]).
Marriage that pleases God must be based on a Spiritual
relationship.

In I Corinthians 7:39 Paul says that a widow may
marry, "only in the Lord." *"The wife is bound by the law
as long as her husband liveth; but if her husband be
dead, she is at liberty to be married to whom she will;
only in the Lord."* In other words, she may be involved
only in a marriage that is made within the Lord's
revealed will. In II Corinthians 6:14 this principle is
applied to all of our relationships, especially to the life-
long relationship of marriage: *"Be ye not unequally yoked
together with unbelievers: for what fellowship hath righteousness with unrighteousness? And what communion
hath light with darkness?"*

🕆 A Relationship Originated by God 🕆

*"And the LORD God caused a deep sleep to fall
upon Adam, and he slept: and he took one of his ribs,
and closed up the flesh instead thereof; And the rib,
which the LORD God had taken from man, made he a
woman, and brought her unto the man"* (Genesis 2:21-
22). It was God who made the woman, and it was God
who presented her to the man. God brought them
together. The institution of marriage is of God.

Ours is the era of the "New Morality." Many are
throwing stones at the marriage relationship today. Paul

said that one of the marks of the end-time would be this very thing. *"Forbidding to marry, and commanding to abstain from meats, which God hath created to be received with thanksgiving of them which believe and know the truth"* (1 Timothy 4:3). God said to Peter, *"What God has created, let no man call unclean."* Marriage is an honorable institution because God is honorable and holy.

🌴 A Relationship Valued by God 🌴

"Marriage is honourable in all, and the bed un-defiled: but whoremongers and adulterers God will judge" (Hebrews 13:4). The word *honorable* means to be dear, precious, valuable. How much do we value our marriages? This will be seen by the amount of effort we put into them. The Bible is clear that God considers marriage to be holy, sacred, precious, and valuable. To be in His perfect will, we will have to put the same priority on our marriage. He said it is undefiled. It is free from dirt, filth, and sin. We need to work toward that pure, holy relationship that He gave us and that we have vowed to perform.

🌴 A Relationship Given by God 🌴

"But every man hath his proper gift of God, one after this manner, and another after that" (I Corinthians 7:7). In the context of the verse Paul is writing both to those who are single and to those who are married. The word *gift* used here means a gift of grace—aid to the undeserving. He says that marriage is a gift of grace to some. To others, God gives the grace to remain single. Either way, the gift is of grace. If marriage is a gift of grace, we will have to rely upon Him everyday. He will have to oversee the relationship and supply the grace that we must have to make the marriage work. Are you depending upon Him daily to give you that grace?

2

Marriage is a
One-Flesh Relationship

"And Adam said, This is now bone of my bones, and flesh of my flesh: she shall be called Woman, because she was taken out of Man. Therefore shall a man leave his father and his mother, and shall cleave unto his wife: and they shall be one flesh" (Genesis 2:23-24).

The Unity of the Relationship

"And Adam gave names to all cattle, and to the fowl of the air, and to every beast of the field; but for Adam there was not found an help meet for him" (Genesis 2:20). Man had a need for a companion. This companion would become his *helpmeet*—his counterpart, opposite, or completion. In God's eyes the man was incomplete until he had a *helpmeet* or completer.

The need was met by divine surgery. *"And the LORD God caused a deep sleep to fall upon Adam, and he slept: and he took one of his ribs, and closed up the flesh instead thereof; and the rib, which the LORD God had taken from man, made he a woman, and brought her unto the man"* (Genesis 2:21-22). God took a rib from Adam, the man, and designed a completer to meet the need.

Adam recognized the fulfillment of the will of God in marriage. *"And Adam said, This is now bone of my* bones, and flesh of my flesh: she shall be called Woman, because she was taken out of Man" (Genesis 2:23). She is called *Woman,* meaning of the man or from the man. Without her, he is incomplete. Without him, she is unfulfilled. The two of them put together make up a whole.

Leaving Parents

Adam, under divine inspiration, said, *"Therefore shall a man leave his father and his mother, and shall cleave unto his wife: and they shall be one flesh"* (Genesis 2:24). Leaving means to loosen, separate, or depart. The pair are a completed whole. There is no need or place for an addition. In fact, any appendage to the completed unit only serves to complicate and confuse God's plan.

The woman is to leave and cleave also. *"Hearken, O daughter, and consider, and incline thine ear; forget also thine own people, and thy father's house"* (Psalm 45:10).

Leaving our parents does not exempt us from the responsibilities to our parents which are Biblical:

We are to honor our parents. *"Honor thy father and mother: that thy days may be long upon the land which the LORD thy God giveth thee"* (Exodus 20:12).

We are to requite (repay) our parents. *"But if any widow have children or nephews, let them learn first to shew piety at home, and to requite their parents: for that is good and acceptable before God"* (1 Timothy 5:4).

We are to follow instructions received as a child. *"My son, hear the instruction of thy father, and forsake not the law of thy mother: for they shall be an ornament of grace unto thy head, and chains about thy neck"* (Proverbs 1:8-9).

Cleaving to Each Other

"Therefore shall a man leave his father and his mother, and shall cleave unto his wife: and they shall be one flesh" (Genesis 2:24). The word *cleave* means to be joined, held fast. It is used to describe the adherence of bone to skin and flesh (Job 19:20), the covering of fish's

flesh with scales (Ezekiel 29:4), the infiltration of disease to the body (Deuteronomy 28:60; II Kings 5:27). In other words, the word *cleave* speaks of the closest possible relationship.

Cleaving and leaving are two sides of the same coin. It is impossible to cleave until you leave. All interfering relationships must be left, and there must be a singleness of heart. Then comes the cleaving. One major obstacle that every newly married couple must overcome is outside interference. Many times the interference is family. It may also be old friends, relationships from the single life, or new friends. All must take second place to the marriage relationship.

🌴 The Uniting of the Relationship 🌴

Uniting the Two Parts of God's Image Into One
"So God created man in his own image, in the image of God created he him; male and female created he them" (Genesis 1:27).

Remember that the woman is the completer of the man. Without the partner, neither is whole. In oneness, the couple reflects the attributes of God. The nature of the woman is the reflection of His image in her compassion (Matthew 9:36), love (I John 4:8), and nurturing (Titus 2:4-5). The nature of the man reflects the image of God as protector (Psalm 91:1-2), leader (Exodus 6:13), and supplier (John 6:32).

Reuniting Adam With His Rib
"And the LORD God caused a deep sleep to fall upon Adam, and he slept: and he took one of his ribs, and closed up the flesh instead thereof; and the rib, which the LORD God had taken from man, made he a woman, and brought her unto the man. And Adam said, This is now bone of my bones, and flesh of my flesh: she shall be called Woman, because she was taken out of Man.

Therefore shall a man cleave unto his wife: and they shall be one flesh" (Genesis 2:21-24).

Intimate Union

"Know ye not that your bodies are the members of Christ? Shall I then take the members of Christ, and make them the members of an harlot? God forbid. What? Know ye not that he which is joined to an harlot is one body? For two, saith he, shall be one flesh" (I Corinthians 6:15-16).

The results of becoming one flesh is fruit—children. *"And God blessed them, and God said unto them, Be fruitful, and multiply, and replenish the earth, and subdue it: and have dominion over the fish of the sea, and over the fowl of the air, and over every living thing that moveth upon the earth"* (Genesis 1:28). This is the outward declaration of leaving and cleaving.

3

Marriage is a
Yoked Relationship

Marriage is a divine relationship: a relationship that pleases God, was originated by God, valued by God, and given by God (Chapter 1).

Marriage is also a one-flesh relationship. There is a unity of the relationship, in which there must be a leaving of other relationships and a cleaving in this relationship. There is also a uniting of the relationship, in which the two become one flesh. This is a work that only God can do. Therefore it is important for Him to have all authority in the marriage (Chapter 2). In this chapter, we will define marriage a little further.

🌲 The Yoked Relationship Defined 🌲

"Be ye not unequally yoked together with unbelievers: for what fellowship hath righteousness with unrighteousness and what communion hath light with darkness?" (II Corinthians 6:14).

The word *unequally* describes the relationship of two individuals who are of different types. One of the individuals is described as an *unbeliever*—one who denies the Christian faith. The word *yoked* means to couple two together. The command expressed in this verse, then, is: "Do not be coupled together with one who is a denier of the faith."

Paul wrote the admonition of II Corinthians 6:14 to the church of Corinth—a church in a wicked place. The members of the church existed in a world full of all the wickedness of Rome. Paul did not write this verse specifically to prospective brides and grooms. It was written to Christians, to be applied to all areas of our lives. In other words, we should not be *unequally yoked with unbelievers* at all. Whether it is in the business world, the social world, or the religious world, this verse applies. It applies to clubs, fishing partners, next-door neighbors, kinfolk, and best friends. As with all of Scripture, it is still applicable to us in this day and time. We are not to be coupled to those that deny the faith.

In a much more serious sense, this admonition applies to those who are entering into a divine, one-flesh relationship. This relationship is possible *"only in the Lord,"* (I Corinthians 7:39). II Corinthians 6:14 emphasizes the impossibility of any other relationship: *"What fellowship hath righteousness with unrighteousness? And what communion hath light with darkness?"* Paul says that righteousness (the removal of all sin through the justification of Jesus Christ) has no fellowship with unrighteousness (transgression of the law, wickedness). He compares the impossibility of light and darkness coming together. It just cannot happen.

There can be no continuance or fulfillment in a coupling that has no relationship. The two can coexist, but they cannot commune. *"Can two walk together, except they be agreed?"* (Amos 3:3).

🌴 The Yoked Relationship's Results 🌴

Several results come from the yoked relationship. Although I believe these to be the results rather than the means of the yoked relationship, they must be recognized and acknowledged mutually. Because of our carnality, they will also have to be worked at mutually.

Total Sharing

Total sharing is one result of a yoked relationship where all things are shared in common in the fellowship of the yoke. Through total intimacy the coexisting pair are brought into communion. They share all things equally and fairly. There are no secrets or surprises. Each is perfectly willing to give up to the other, because of the yoking that is involved. This yoking calls for total agreement in the planning and goals of the marriage with no independent goals. Since each is dependent upon the other for success and happiness, the yoked pair must set out in the same direction. This is only accomplished by mutual submission to the Lord. *"Submitting yourselves one to another in the fear of God"* (Ephesians 5:21).

Since the yoked pair totally share all things in the relationship and are headed in the same direction, there is no independent labor. All their labor is for their mutual benefit. This does not negate the division of responsibilities. There will still be areas that are primarily his and primarily hers, but each area is worked for the common good. Thus both will benefit from the other's labor, and each should be willing to assist as necessary.

Total Harmony

Another result of a yoked relationship is harmony. Harmony does not mean that we sing the same part, but that your alto or soprano harmonizes with my bass. It is that we are in one accord, unison, or agreement. In the yoked relationship, all is shared in harmony. Although each is an individual, each is in harmony with the Lord and with the other.

*What therefore God hath
joined together,
let not man put asunder.*
Matthew 19:6

*Dr. Wayne Hudson emphasized the covenant of
marriage in the wedding of Chip and Mary Stock,
June 23, 2001, at Bayou Drive Baptist Church. Chip
and Mary and their little daughter Bethany now live
in Bartlesville, Oklahoma.*

4

Marriage is a Covenant Relationship

"Yet ye say, Wherefore? Because the LORD hath been witness between thee and the wife of thy youth, against whom thou hast dealt treacherously: yet is she thy companion, and the wife of thy covenant" (Malachi 2:14).

🌴 The Promise of the Covenant 🌴

The word *covenant* means an agreement or treaty between two parties. To be valid, the Biblical covenant requires a witness, sometimes a third person. A good example is the covenant agreement made by Boaz and the near kinsman before the elders in the story of Ruth: *"And Boaz said unto the elders, and unto all the people, Ye are witnesses this day, that I have bought all that was Elimelech's, and all that Chilion's and Mahlon's, of the hand of Naomi"* (Ruth 4:9).

At other times, a token becomes the witness of the covenant. An example is the token of circumcision given with God's covenant to Abraham in Genesis 17:6-11.

🌴 The Partners of the Covenant 🌴

The Consenting Parties

As in other covenants, there are two parties who commit to the promise (treaty or agreement) of the covenant. The marital agreement is the covenant (voluntary promise) between the man and the woman. The man and the woman become companions who are knit together by promise. The promise is made from heart to heart. It is a life-long commitment of heart. It is a promise of honor.

The Covenant Witness

There must also be a witness to the covenant. God is the witness to the promise that is made in the marital agreement. Only He affirms the covenant of marriage. He holds both parties responsible to keep their part of the covenant.

"And this have ye done again, covering the altar of the LORD with tears, with weeping, and with crying out, insomuch that he regardeth not the offering any more, or receiveth it with good will at your hand. Yet ye say, Wherefore? Because the LORD hath been witness between thee and the wife of thy youth, against whom thou hast dealt treacherously: yet is she thy companion, and the wife of thy covenant. And did not he make one? Yet had he the residue of the spirit. And wherefore one? That he might seek a godly seed. Therefore take heed to your spirit, and let none deal treacherously against the wife of his youth. For the LORD, the God of Israel, saith that he hateth putting away: for one covereth violence with his garment, saith the LORD of hosts: therefore take heed to your spirit, that ye deal not treacherously" (Malachi 2:13-16).

The marriage covenant is called the "covenant of God;" i.e. the covenant that God recognizes. (It is not "the covenant with God." That is the covenant made at salvation.) Because of the witness of the covenant, the promise made takes on special significance. It is a holy promise, made before a Holy God.

The Covenant Commemoration

The marriage ceremony is the public declaration of the covenant (voluntary promise) that has already been made, or will be made, in the hearts of a man and woman. The marriage license becomes the written witness to the promise that has been made. These then become the "tokens" of the covenant.

🌴 The Divine Power of the Covenant 🌴

The Covenant of Holy Matrimony is:

Instituted by God

God values marriage. He said, *"It is not good that the man should be alone; I will make him an help meet for him"* (Genesis 2:18). Then He began the institution of marriage: *"And the rib, which the LORD God had taken from man, made he a woman, and brought her unto the man"* (Genesis 2:22).

Governed by God

Paul's instructions to wives, husbands, children, fathers, and servants in Colossians 3:16-23 are replete with the words, *"As it is fit in the Lord," "well pleasing to the Lord," "fearing God";* they conclude with this important admonition, *"And whatsoever ye do, do it heartily, as to the Lord, and not to men."*

Blessed by God

As with all other areas of our lives, God's blessings are upon obedience to His Word and will. The Bible certainly promises His blessings upon Godly families. He will always bless the marriage that is committed to Him.

Sanctioned by God

To the Old Testament saints, God promised to judge unto the third and fourth generations those who worshipped idols. The judgments of God as well as the blessings of God to children are largely determined by parental behavior. In our day, the rebellion of young people and its consequences are directly attributable to the breakdown of marriages and homes.

Concluded by God

Because it is a covenant relationship, and because the covenant is made in the presence of God's witness, it is a life-long commitment. Man is not to break the covenant made before God. Jesus said, *"What therefore God hath joined together, let not man put asunder"* (Matthew 19:6).

5

Marriage is Lawful, Temporal, and Symbolic

🌴 Marriage is a Lawful Relationship 🌴

Controlled and Regulated by God's laws

The woman is bound by God's laws. *"The wife is bound by the law as long as her husband liveth; but if her husband be dead, she is at liberty to be married to whom she will; only in the Lord"* (I Corinthians 7:39).

The man is also bound by God's laws. *"Art thou bound unto a wife? seek not to be loosed. Art thou loosed from a wife? seek not a wife"* (I Corinthians 7:27).

To be *bound by the law* is to be under the power or authority of the law. The word *bound* literally means to tie or bind together. Perhaps this is where we get the expression "tying the knot." Biblically, God's laws bind the marriage participants to a responsibility to God's Word and will.

To Be Lived in Accordance with God's Laws

Marriage is a union that is regulated by God's laws. To please God, our married life must be lived in accordance with God's laws.

🌴 Marriage is a Temporal Relationship 🌴

Marriage Lasts Only for the Course of Our Lifetime

"For in the resurrection they neither marry, nor are

given in marriage, but are as the angels of God in heaven" (Matthew 22:30).

Jesus told the Sadducees, *"there is no marriage in Heaven."* As we have seen, marriage is an agreement that is effective upon the earth. Marriage is only temporal. There will be no need of procreation, no lust of the flesh, no need for two to be united to perfectly reveal Christ in heaven (glorified bodies, I John 3:2), nor any need of companionship, for we will *"ever be with the Lord"* (I Thessalonians 4:17).

🌳 Marriage Is A Symbolic Relationship 🌳

The Bible gives two relationships that are personified in the marriage relationship.

God the Father and National Israel

"For thy Maker is thine husband; the LORD of hosts is his name; and thy Redeemer the Holy One of Israel; The God of the whole earth shall he be called" (Isaiah 54:5).

"Turn, O backsliding children, saith the LORD; for I am married unto you: and I will take you one of a city, and two of a family, and I will bring you to Zion:" (Jeremiah 3:14).

God the Son and the Local Church

"For the husband is the head of the wife, even as Christ is the head of the church: and he is the saviour of the body. Therefore as the church is subject unto Christ, so let the wives be to their own husbands in every thing. Husbands, love your wives, even as Christ also loved the church, and gave himself for it; that he might sanctify and cleanse it with the washing of water by the word, that he might present it to himself a glorious church, not having spot, or wrinkle, or any such thing; but that it should be holy and without blemish. So ought men to love their wives as their own bodies. He that loveth his wife loveth himself. For no man ever yet hated his own flesh; but nourisheth and cherisheth it, even as the Lord the church: For we are

members of his body, of his flesh, and of his bones. For this cause shall a man leave his father and mother, and shall be joined unto his wife, and they two shall be one flesh. This is a great mystery: but I speak concerning Christ and the church" (Ephesians 5:23-32). The Song of Solomon also shows this relationship in the types of the Shulamite maiden and the Shepherd Prince.

The only way that the marriage relationship will ever measure up to Biblical standards is for every marriage participant to cast himself or herself upon the grace of God. As with all other areas of life the very first requirement for a successful marriage is that both parties must be born again. Then, as with all other areas of Christian life, the requirement is to be filled, motivated, and empowered by the Holy Spirit. Of ourselves we have no power to live in His pattern. Only by the help of the Holy Spirit will we be able to overcome the world, the flesh, and the devil.

Will you now ask Him, and allow Him to control your life and your marriage relationship?

6

Marriage is a Perfect Relationship

Let's investigate the last of the descriptions of the marriage relationship. Please remember that is impossible for these relationships to be discussed in fullness and completeness here. In addition, these principles are not to be learned by definition only. They are in the Scripture, so we must put them into practice in our homes as the Holy Spirit enables us.

"And when I passed by thee, and saw thee polluted in thine own blood, I said unto thee when thou wast in thy blood, Live; yea, I said unto thee when thou wast in thy blood, Live. I have caused thee to multiply as the bud of the field, and thou hast increased and waxen great, and thou art come to excellent ornaments: thy breasts are fashioned, and thine hair is grown, whereas thou wast naked and bare. Now when I passed by thee, and looked upon thee, behold, thy time was the time of love; and I spread my skirt over thee, and covered thy nakedness: yea, I sware unto thee, and entered into a covenant with thee, saith the Lord GOD, and thou becamest mine. Then washed I thee with water; yea, I thoroughly washed away thy blood from thee, and I anointed thee with oil. I clothed thee also with broidered work, and shod thee with badgers' skin, and I girded thee about with fine linen, and I covered thee with silk. I decked thee also

with ornaments, and I put bracelets upon thy hands, and a chain on thy neck. And I put a jewel on thy forehead, and earrings in thine ears, and a beautiful crown upon thine head. Thus wast thou decked with gold and silver; and thy raiment was of fine linen, and silk, and broidered work; thou didst eat fine flour, and honey, and oil: and thou wast exceeding beautiful, and thou didst prosper into a kingdom. And thy renown went forth among the heathen for thy beauty: for it was perfect through my comeliness, which I had put upon thee, saith the Lord GOD" (Ezekiel 16:6-14).

This passage in Ezekiel is written from the viewpoint of God, with regard to the marriage relationship, as He speaks of His relationship with Israel. The principles of the passage reveal a perfect relationship, for they are established by God Himself.

Ezekiel 16:6-7 speaks of the day that He found His spouse. She was polluted, weak, and very unlovely. He loved her in spite of her deficiencies. He did not love her because of how she looked. Marriage is not built upon the finding of strengths. Biblical marriage is a relationship that is strong in spite of weaknesses. True love is not dependent upon appearance.

This is contrary to all that Hollywood and television teach our society today. The world says, "Look for the beautiful person, for in that beauty you will find happiness." Of course, each of us should do the best we can to be attractive to the eye of our mate, but beauty has little to do with happiness. Consider the so-called "beautiful people;" look at their divorce rate and look at their suicide rate. Beauty does not equate with happiness; godliness equates with happiness.

Ezekiel 16:9-14 speaks of the continual care and exaltation of the marriage partner. God said that He washed and cared for the weaker one. He gave unto her what was needed for health and life. Out of His own love He met her need.

He then gave gifts of jewels, ornaments of gold, fine clothing, and fine foods for the perfecting of His loved one. It is a picture of the sacrifice of true love. Love is an action word. True love is sacrificial for the edification of the loved one. The result of this kind of love is seen in verse 14: *"And thy renown went forth among the heathen for thy beauty: for it was perfect through my comeliness, which I had put upon thee, saith the Lord GOD."*

If you want happiness and contentment in marriage, build up one another. The beauty of the person who is esteemed by his or her mate grows until it is seen by others—but it is built by self-sacrifice. Selfish interests have no place in the marriage relationship. If left unchecked, they will destroy the relationship and the individual.

In the center of all these verses is a beautiful picture of the marriage relationship. *"Now when I passed by thee, and looked upon thee, behold, thy time was the time of love; and I spread my skirt over thee, and covered thy nakedness: yea, I sware unto thee, and entered into a covenant with thee, saith the Lord GOD, and thou becamest mine"* (Ezekiel 16:8). Several principles of a biblical marriage relationship are found here:

Now when I passed by thee, and looked upon thee— The choosing of one another. This is critical in a successful marriage relationship.

Behold, thy time was the time of love—Love for one another. The basis for Scriptural marriage is love for one another, within the will of God.

And I spread my skirt over thee, and covered thy nakedness—Proof of love, giving of self for the other. True love involves protection, care, and the taking of shame. Never does true love involve abuse, misuse, or the causing of shame.

Yea, I sware unto thee, and entered into a covenant with thee, saith the Lord GOD—The marriage covenant is made. It is a covenant between two people and is made as a holy vow before the Lord.

And thou becamest mine—The cleaving, or the possession of one another. Marriage partners no longer live for themselves alone. The spouse is now a part of them and must be considered at all times.

Photo:

Keith and Natalie Richard were married at Bayou Drive Baptist Church, April 11, 1992. Keith and Natalie are still members of Bayou Drive Baptist Church and are raising their three daughters for the Lord.

Part Two

Biblical Marriage Responsibilities

*Therefore shall a man leave his father
and his mother, and shall cleave unto his wife.*
Genesis 2:24

7

The Authority of the Couple

In previous chapters we have investigated the marriage relationship in the light of the Bible. Going further, I would like to look at some Bible principles of responsibilities that need to be in place in the Christian home. All these principles are given in simplicity and austerity. Most are presented in outline form and to the point. The details and individual application are left for you and your own situation.

All authority involves responsibility. This is true with both the husband's and the wife's authority. They must prayerfully exercise their authority in a proper way, with love and restraint.

🌳 The Husband's Authority 🌳

The Husband's Authority is as the Leader of the Family.

"Even as Sara obeyed Abraham, calling him lord: whose daughters ye are, as long as ye do well, and are not afraid with any amazement" (I Peter 3:6). This verse is puzzling to many and offensive to some. To a great degree this principle has been abused, particularly among fundamentalists. Regardless of all the controversy, it is a Biblical principle and we need to seek understanding and adherence to it. The word *lord*

means master, ruler, the possessor of authority. To obey is to listen to, then attend to the instructions of, to fulfill the needs of.

"But I would have you know, that the head of every man is Christ; and the head of the woman is the man; and the head of Christ is God" (I Corinthians 11:3). The word *head* literally means head. He is to be the instructor and the decision maker. Of course, *head* implies being a listener. The husband should always listen to the wife's desires and suggestions and take them into account. However, the authority and responsibility for all final decisions rest upon him.

The husband is not placed as head of the household due to any inherent ability to be a better leader. God has simply planned the home this way. In His sovereignty, He has designated a decision maker for the home. Every player on a football team does not call the plays. That is the responsibility of the quarterback. This does not mean that he is a better athlete or smarter. It is simply the authority that goes with his position. A man needs to listen to the advice of a godly wife because she has great wisdom. The wife, notwithstanding her wisdom and abilities, submits to her husband as leader of the family as an act of faith.

🌳 The Wife's Authority 🌳

The Wife's Authority is as Leader of the Household.

The Bible gives at least four areas of authority and responsibility of the wife in the household.

She supervises the household.

"She looketh well to the ways of her household, and eateth not the bread of idleness" (Proverbs 31:27). *She looketh well*—This is not so much the cooking and cleaning of the household. It is the thought process that is required to oversee the household. Two areas are implied by the verse: the mental activity required to

administer the household, and the physical activity required to properly care for the household.

She strengthens the household.

"Every wise woman buildeth her house: but the foolish plucketh it down with her hands" (Proverbs 14:1). Anything that is harmful to the household is off-limits. Her primary concern is the building of her household. Everything done within the household should be for the benefit of her family and according to the Lord's will.

She supports the household.

"I will therefore that the younger women marry, bear children, guide the house, give none occasion to the adversary to speak reproachfully" (I Timothy 5:14). She is the administrator of the home. That is, she guides the home according to the Bible policies and the standards set by her husband. In the home, he could be referred to as the "director of the board" who sets a policy. The wife is the "executive" who sees that the policies are practiced. Wife, what an opportunity you have to establish and administrate your home in such a way that it becomes the sweet-smelling savor of Christ.

She stands watch over the household.

"To be discreet, chaste, keepers at home, good, obedient to their own husbands, that the word of God be not blasphemed" (Titus 2:5). She is like the middle-eastern shepherd who stayed with the flock. He was aware of the dangers and needs of the sheep because he lived with them. He knew them individually. Jesus said that a *hireling* would not do this. No babysitter or daycare can take the place of a mother. The nurturing, protecting and guarding of the household is in capable hands when the wife and mother fulfils her responsibility and takes her authority.

*The head of every man is Christ;
and the head of the woman is the
man; and the head of Christ is God.*
I Corinthians 11:3

*Pastor Wayne and Mrs. Susie Hudson at
the celebration of their 40th wedding
anniversary, December 9, 2001.*

8

The Submission
of the Couple

Along with authority in a relationship (Chapter 7), there is always a need for submission. This subject of submission immediately raises a flag. It has been misstated and misunderstood by many. I ask you to clear any preconceived ideas from your mind and approach this subject prayerfully.

🌲 The Submission of the Husband 🌲

"But I would have you know, that the head of every man is Christ; and the head of the woman is the man; and the head of Christ is God" (I Corinthians 11:3). Many people, quick to emphasize the submission of the wife, completely neglect the submission of the husband. Although I had heard much preaching about the submission of the wife to the husband, it was not until I began to study the subject in the Bible that I understood that God intends for the husband to submit also.

He Must Submit to Christ
The word *head* is used three times in I Corinthians 11:3 and means a literal head in comparison to the body. The head is the decision maker for the body. For the husband, this head is Christ.

He Mutually Submits to His Wife
"Submitting yourselves one to another in the fear of

God" (Ephesians 5:21). While he has the headship for his family, the husband, as a Christian, is bound to submit to others. This is a natural result of the love and peace that is produced by the indwelling of Christ through the Holy Spirit. He is bound by the Spirit of Him who *"When he was reviled, he reviled not again"* (I Peter 2:23).

Colossians 3 emphasizes that all our temporal relationships are measured and motivated by Christ. *"But Christ is all, and in all. Put on therefore, as the elect of God, holy and beloved, bowels of mercies, kindness, humbleness of mind, meekness, long-suffering; Forbearing one another, and forgiving one another, if any man have a quarrel against any: even as Christ forgave you, so also do ye. And above all these things put on charity, which is the bond of perfectness. And let the peace of God rule in your hearts, to the which also ye are called in one body; and be ye thankful"* (Colossians 3:11-15). Continuing, Paul lays the guidelines for relationships, both in the home and out of the home. He concludes the passage with these words: *"And whatsoever ye do, do it heartily, as to the Lord, and not unto men"* (Colossians 3:23).

🌴 The Submission Of The Wife 🌴

She Must Submit to Christ

"Favour is deceitful, and beauty is vain: but a woman that feareth the LORD, she shall be praised" (Proverbs 31:30).

Favour—Kindness that is brought about by ability to get pity.

Deceitful—Deception that results in disappointment .

Beauty—The properties which make a person pleasing and desirable.

Vain—Worthless, of no lasting value.

Fear of the Lord—A reverence that results in action. It is brought about by knowledge of another's greatness and one's own weakness.

There has probably never been a day in which a woman is pressured in the areas of favor and beauty as much as she is today. Most women look upon the acceptance of others, based upon worldly standards, as success. Others spend all their energies and spare no expense to be looked upon as beautiful. The book of God's wisdom says both of these efforts are of no lasting value. It is a life of submission (fear of the Lord) that produces lasting success.

The verses quoted here, Ephesians 5:21 and Colossians 3:11-15, are directed toward a wife as well as toward the husband. She is to submit herself to Christ also.

She Must Submit to Her Husband

"Wives, submit yourselves unto your own husbands, as unto the Lord. For the husband is the head of the wife, even as Christ is the head of the church: and he is the saviour of the body. Therefore as the church is subject unto Christ, so let the wives be to their own husbands in every thing" (Ephesians 5:22-24).

The two words *submit* and *subject* are from the same Greek word, meaning to rank under, to willfully be under obedience to him because of his position. Theologically, Ephesians 5:24 helps us to understand this concept. It is as the church is motivated by the love of Christ that the church is subject to Christ. Of course, no man will ever love his wife as Jesus loves His church. But where love is the motivation, submission is not a problem.

Why Must the Woman Submit to the Man?

"Let the woman learn in silence with all subjection. But I suffer not a woman to teach, nor to usurp authority over the man, but to be in silence. For Adam was first formed, then Eve. And Adam was not deceived, but the woman being deceived was in the transgression" (I Timothy 2:11-14).

God created Eve to be a helpmeet (one who aids) for Adam. *"And the LORD God said, It is not good that the man should be alone; I will make him an help meet for him"* (Genesis 2:18). Eve was deceived. *"And Adam was not deceived, but the woman being deceived was in the transgression"* (I Timothy 2:14).

Eve was beguiled—totally deceived. *"But I fear, lest by any means, as the serpent beguiled Eve through his subtlety, so your minds should be corrupted from the simplicity that is in Christ"* (II Corinthians 11:3). Eve, when separated from her husband's protection and authority, was easily tempted and persuaded.

Adam was to *rule;* that was God's plan. *"Unto the woman he said, I will greatly multiply thy sorrow and thy conception; in sorrow thou shalt bring forth children; and thy desire shall be to thy husband, and he shall rule over thee"* (Genesis 3:16).

Does all this mean that the husband is better than the wife in any way? Absolutely not. What it does mean is that God designed and decreed a different position of responsibility for the husband and the wife. She is unique and irreplaceable in her position; likewise he in his position. One is not better or smarter. Many times she may be smarter or more talented. But, they are set in the Christian home by rank. Submission, on the part of each, is accepting God's plan for the home. It is only accepted by faith, but when accepted, it is sure to bring God's blessings on that home.

9

The Attitude
of the Couple

None of the other characteristics of the marriage relationship will be effective if the husband and wife have wrong attitudes toward one another.

🌲 The Attitude of the Husband 🌲

He Values His Wife

"Likewise, ye husbands, dwell with them according to knowledge, giving honour unto the wife, as unto the weaker vessel, and as being heirs together of the grace of life; that your prayers be not hindered" (I Peter 3:7).

According to knowledge—By knowledge of the Word.

Giving honor—To value.

Weaker vessel—Without equal strength, both physically and emotionally.

Heirs together—Completely equal in the family of God, in the grace of God, in Christian life, and in eternal rewards.

Prayers be not hindered—In order for the relationship with God to be right, there must be no known sin. *"Behold, the LORD's hand is not shortened, that it cannot save; neither his ear heavy, that it cannot hear: But your iniquities have separated between you and your God, and your sins have hid his face from you, that he will not hear"* (Isaiah 59:1-2). God indicates that a lack of harmony in the marital relationship is a sin and must be corrected in order to keep a right relationship with Him.

"So ought men to love their wives as their own bodies. He that loveth his wife loveth himself. For no man ever yet hated his own flesh; but nourisheth and cherisheth it, even as the Lord the church" (Ephesians 5:28-29).

He is to value her as he values himself, to care for her needs as he cares for himself. His focus must be shifted from "self alone" to "her as himself." This goes back to the "one flesh" principle, which has already been discussed. The wife *is* the husband and the husband *is* the wife.

Nourisheth—To attend, so as to cause growth.

Cherisheth—To give warmth, comfort, protection. This word literally means to set upon, as a hen sacrificially sets upon her brood of young.

He Seeks His Wife's Welfare

Praise

"Her children arise up, and call her blessed; her husband also, and he praiseth her" (Proverbs 31:28). Probably one of the most neglected principles is the praise of a faithful spouse. To praise means to make shine. One of the most encouraging things anyone can hear is an honest word of praise. To take for granted those whom God has blessed us with is a common trap.

Trust

"The heart of her husband doth safely trust in her, so that he shall have no need of spoil" (Proverbs 31:11). To trust is to believe, not to question. Trust is built over time, but there can be no harmony in the marriage relationship outside of an attitude of trust.

Spoil means to gain by force. In a Biblical marriage, the husband does not have to rule by force. He will trust her to do what is proper in any given situation.

Honesty

"Yet ye say, Wherefore? Because the LORD hath been witness between thee and the wife of thy youth, against whom thou hast dealt treacherously: yet is she thy companion, and the wife of thy covenant. And did not he make one? Yet had he the residue of the spirit. And wherefore one? That he might seek a godly seed. Therefore take heed to your spirit, and let none deal treacherously against the wife of his youth. For the LORD, the God of Israel, saith that he hateth putting away: for one covereth violence with his garment, saith the LORD of hosts: therefore take heed to your spirit, that ye deal not treacherously" (Malachi 2:14-16).

In this passage God is speaking to a people who have regarded the marriage vow lightly. Putting away a wife for any reason has become readily accepted. God gives a warning about dealing *treacherously.* We live in such a day.

The word *treacherously* means to deal hypocritically, harmfully, unfaithfully; not in a trustworthy manner. This passage, although written to men, strikes at a root problem in the attitude of both husbands and wives. As Christians, our goal should be to deal honestly with all men. *"That ye may walk honestly toward them that are without, and that ye may have lack of nothing"* (I Thessalonians 4:12). How much more this should apply in our dealings with our spouse. God says that he hates the sin of dishonesty: *"For the LORD, the God of Israel, saith that he hateth putting away: for one covereth violence with his garment, saith the LORD of hosts"* (Malachi 2:16). He then gives a warning: *"Therefore take heed to your spirit, that ye deal not treacherously."*

In a day when adulterous affairs, flirtations, and unnatural desires are so prevalent, every husband needs to meditate upon these verses and rethink his attitude toward the one whom God has given him. Considering the confidence of God and your wife, determine to have a right attitude toward your marriage now before the temptation comes.

🌴 The Attitude of the Wife 🌴

She Reverences Her Husband

"*Nevertheless let every one of you in particular so love his wife even as himself; and the wife see that she reverence her husband*" (Ephesians 5:33). *Reverence* means to stand in awe of. Granted, ladies, most of your husbands are not too awesome. But, God has placed your husband in the marriage to be just that to you. He is to be your partner in fellowship, responsibility, heartaches, victories, and intimacy. He is to be your provider. Of course, he has responsibility for your physical well-being, but he is to provide mental support and spiritual leadership as well.

In the home, the husband and father is to be the representative of God. As such, he must have your reverence. Of course, many husbands will fail in this, but we are discussing the attitude of the wife right now. It is not the man that is to be reverenced, it is the husband. It is not the person, it is his position of responsibility. Though we may strongly disagree with and have little respect for certain political leaders because of their personal misconduct, the Scriptures mandate that we honor them in their positions of leadership.

The husband is to be the wife's protector. The Scripture is very clear in pronouncing the wife to be the *weaker vessel.* In the Garden of Eden, it was Eve who was deceived. It appears that she was vulnerable to the deception of Satan. Adam sinned willfully. God has given him the responsibility and the ability of spiritual leadership. Instead of rebellion or ridicule, the wife should be thankful for, supportive of, and reverential toward the husband God has given her. By attitude, many wives seem to say, "I do not need a partner, a provider, or a protector." Don't fall into this trap.

She Seeks Her Husband's Welfare

"*A virtuous woman is a crown to her husband: but she that maketh ashamed is as rottenness in his bones*" (Proverbs 12:4).

Virtuous—To give strength or to bring strength; indicates actions which will bring strength or cause strength to be increased.

Ashamed—The paleness caused by fear; the action that causes fearfulness.

I doubt that any wife truly understands her power to strengthen her husband. Someone has well said, "Behind every great man there is a great woman." Wife, if you want to prosper, to be a winner, to know the blessing of God on your marriage, learn to act in a way that causes your husband to be stronger, not weaker. Instead of discouraging him and tearing him down in your conversation, learn to encourage and build him up. You may be surprised at the results. Since you are a part of him, whatever he becomes, whether victorious or a failure, you will share.

Proverbs 31:12 says, "*She will do him good and not evil all the days of her life.*" To *do him good* means to exercise proper action resulting in praise. To do *evil* is to harm, render useless, to break into pieces. The Biblical attitude for every wife, regardless of her circumstances, is to *do him good*. You may say, "You don't know what he has done." That's true, but God knows and knew before the world was created or the Bible was written. He says *do him good*. How long? *All the days of her life.* It is not for the wife to "get even." She is simply to *do him good*.

One of the great fallacies of the present generation is that of self-gratification. Nothing is more detrimental to the marriage relationship. In this area of attitude toward your spouse, don't be trapped into fantasies or comparisons with other husbands. What you married is what you have for life. Do your best to build him up, then pray that God would make him the man you need.

I realize that the principles guiding the attitudes of the husband and wife found in this chapter do not match up with present day thinking or practice, but they do not come from a sociology book or a psychology book. These attitudes come from God's Book. I urge you today to check your attitude toward your spouse compared to the teaching of the Bible.

1 0

The Emotions
of the Couple

In previous chapters we have looked at several aspects of the responsibilities of the couple: the authority of the couple, their submission and their attitudes. Although each of these areas produces action, none of them has action in themselves. When all these areas are properly in place, performing our God-given responsibilities will be the natural result. Let's look at one more of these stage-setting areas: the emotions of the husband and wife.

🌴 The Emotions of the Husband 🌴

Find Joy in Your Wife

"*Live joyfully with the wife whom thou lovest all the days of the life of thy vanity, which he hath given thee under the sun, all the days of thy vanity: for that is thy portion in this life, and in thy labour which thou takest under the sun*" (Ecclesiastes 9:9). *Live joyfully*—to look upon with joy, to experience joy, to see joy. This verse admonishes the husband to look upon his wife with joy in his heart. Husband, do you experience this emotion as you think upon, look upon, experience life with your wife? Solomon says, by divine inspiration, that this is your lot in life. This should erase comparisons, dissatisfaction, and lusts for all others. Since this is your lot in life, it benefits you to find joy in your wife and your marriage.

Love Your wife

"*Husbands, love your wives, and be not bitter against them*" (Colossians 3:19). The word *love* used here is from the Greek word *agapao*, which is the strongest, widest, and most far-reaching word for love in the Bible. This is the **all-encompassing love** which God showed for the world: "*For God so loved the world that he gave his only begotten son, that whosoever believeth in him should not perish, but have everlasting life*" (John 3:16). It is the **self-sacrificing love** which Jesus has for the church: "*Husbands, love your wives, even as Christ also loved the church, and gave himself for it*" (Ephesians 5:25). It is the **never-failing love** that Paul describes in I Corinthians 13. It can only be "*the love of God that is shed abroad in our hearts by the Holy Ghost*" (Romans 5:5).

You may be wondering, "Why so much emphasis upon the **Christian** home?" Outside of the saving grace of the Lord Jesus, an all-encompassing, self-sacrificing, never-failing love is impossible for any husband to attain. You cannot be the husband, the wife, or the parent God intends you to be without being saved, set apart, and Spirit-led. Then, as a Christian you must maintain a constant close relationship with the Lord (not a walk of the natural, but of the supernatural— indeed, the spiritual). Out of this relationship is born the type of love that you need in your marriage.

Have No Bitterness Toward Your Wife

"*And be not bitter against them*" (Colossians 3:19). The word *bitter*, as used here, is a verb meaning to embitter, to make bitter, to irritate or prick. Bitterness is described in Hebrews 12:15 as a root. "*Looking diligently lest any man fall of the grace of God; lest any root of bitterness springing up trouble you, and thereby many be defiled.*" The root of bitterness will produce the fruit of bitterness. Hebrews describes the fruit of bitterness as a stain. It will affect all those around you.

But in the end you are the one who is troubled by it. Husband, search your heart to root out all bitterness and replace it with *agape* love. Instead of irritating or embittering your wife, you should comfort your wife. *"Then said Elkanah her husband to her, Hannah, why weepest thou? And why eatest thou not? And why is thy heart grieved? Am not I better to thee than ten sons?"* (I Samuel 1:8).

🌴 The Emotions of the Wife 🌴

Love Your Husband

"That they may teach the young women to be sober, to love their husbands, to love their children" (Titus 2:4). The word here is love for husband. *Agapao* does not apply—rather, it is *philandros*. *Philandros* means to be affectionate, to show affection, to be loving with warmth to the husband. This is the only place in the New Testament that this word is used.

This love is a self-sacrificing love. This love gives itself to others, to husband and to children. The love of self-sacrifice is probably demonstrated more clearly in the mother-child relationship than any other place in this world, but that same self-sacrificing love is to be given to the husband.

Be Gentle Toward Your Husband

"But let it be the hidden man of the heart, in that which is not corruptible, even the ornament of a meek and quiet spirit, which is in the sight of God of great price" (I Peter 3:4). To be *meek* is to be mild, gentle, or humble. Peter is speaking of the adorning of a wife in I Peter 3:3: *"Whose adorning let it not be that outward adorning of plaiting the hair, and of wearing of gold, or of putting on of apparel."* The single most desirable emotion in a wife, in God's eyes, is that *meek and quiet spirit.* Wife, He says to adorn yourself with this spirit. In other words, this is

a spirit that you can cultivate. When you do, you will be attractive to your husband. More importantly, you will be valuable to God.

As I searched the Scriptures on this subject, I noticed that the burden of cultivating the right emotion is on the husband. I wondered if that is because the husband is not, by nature, an emotional person. Likewise, the admonition to the wife concerning a meek and quiet spirit is a controlling of emotions. This is to the partner who, generally speaking, is ruled by her emotions. In both cases, to be what God requires will take effort and work.

11

The Morality
of the Couple

🌲 The Morality of the Husband 🌲

The Lord is First in All Things

"If any man come to me, and hate not his father, and mother, and wife, and children, and brethren, and sisters, yea, and his own life also, he cannot be my disciple" (Luke 14:26). The word *hate*, as it is used in this passage, means to love less, to be without love. That is, a man's love for wife, parents, children, brother, sister, or any other, in comparison to his love for Christ, is like no love at all.

Paul recognized the tendency for a husband to put his wife first. *"But he that is married careth for the things that are of the world, how he may please his wife"* (I Corinthians 7:33). He uses this as a point of reproach to the believer. Because of his knowledge of her desire for things of the world, the husband's attention is turned from Christ to her desires. The warning is to be sure that your love for Christ supercedes all other loves.

Wife, if the thought of your husband putting God first makes you nervous, understand this. You will never be more loved and honored than by a husband who has made Jesus Lord of all that he is. When he has been motivated by the love of Christ, you will come to a special place that few wives ever attain. Neither husband nor wife can properly love anyone until the love of Christ is shed abroad in his or her heart.

Living is by the Word, Always

"*Likewise, ye husbands, dwell with them according to knowledge, giving honour unto the wife, as unto the weaker vessel, and as being heirs together of the grace of life; that your prayers be not hindered*" (I Peter 3:7). Every decision and action is to be governed by the Word of God. It behooves the Christian husband to saturate himself with the Word of God so that he makes no mistake in the relationship with his wife. Of course, the knowledge of the Word must be put into practice in daily down-to-earth living. In doing so, the husband gives honor to the wife and has the promise of access to the power of God in answered prayers.

Looking to the Needs of Family: Provision

But if any provide not for his own, and specially for those of his own house, he hath denied the faith, and is worse than an infidel" (I Timothy 5:8). Proper provision (*provide*—to direct attention and service to) for the family does not just involve material supplies. It involves giving attention and love as well. In reality, it is the giving of one's self. Provision will require discernment in the giving and the withholding. The decision is dependent upon what is best for the family. There are times when it actually harms someone to satisfy material desires.

Dad, no one else on earth can provide for the needs of your family to the extent that you can. Materially, emotionally, and spiritually, you are appointed to this responsibility. Don't fail those who trust in you. Don't fail the one who has entrusted you with this great privilege. Let God direct you as you lead your family.

By the above verse, if a saved husband does not supply the needs of his family, he does two things. He displays a lack of regard for the Word of God. Additionally, the verse says, he does harm to his testimony, more so than an unbeliever who neglects the needs of his family. God calls upon the husband to be the provider for his family.

May the Word of God be the guide for all we do as parents. It is not a psychologist or sociologist that sets the home in motion. It is God Himself. Who better to direct us toward excellence in our homes?

The Morality of the Wife

She Exercises Godly Wisdom, Always

"...And the contentions of a wife are a continual dropping. House and riches are the inheritance of fathers: and a prudent wife is from the LORD" (Proverbs 19:13-14). The word *prudent* means to be made circumspect, thus, to cause to be Biblically wise, to cause a behavioral change, to be guided wittingly in actions. In Proverbs 31:26, "*She openeth her mouth with wisdom; and in her tongue is the law of kindness,*" the key word is *wisdom* and refers to the use of her mouth.

In these two areas it seems that God is saying, "Let me remake you in my pattern and will, then you will be wise and prudent. This requires a humble, honest application to the Word of God and to prayer.

She Desires Peace With Her Husband

"And the contentions of a wife are a continual dropping" (Proverbs 19:13). To be contentious means to verbally argue a case, to cause discord and strife by a quarrel. Even if you know that you are right, it is sometimes better to keep quiet and to keep peace.

"It is better to dwell in the corner of the housetop, than with a brawling woman and in a wide house." *Brawling* means to be antagonistic, always in disagreement, looking for a fight. These are the works of the flesh (Galatians 5). These works need to be crucified. The Spirit-filled Christian is running over with "*love, joy, peace, longsuffering, gentleness, goodness, faith, meekness, and temperance"* (Galatians 5:22,23). That is the means of peace in the home.

She has a Pleasing Character

"The aged women likewise, that they be in behaviour as becometh holiness, not false accusers, not given to much wine, teachers of good things; that they may teach the young women to be sober, to love their husbands, to love their children. To be discreet, chaste, keepers at home, good, obedient to their own husbands, that the word of God be not blasphemed."

Characteristics that God finds peasing:

Discrete—To be self-controlled. The same word is translated temperate also.

Chaste—To be pure, clean, or perfect. The Hebrew word *hagnos* comes from the root word *hagios,* which is translated holy, i.e. purity that is pleasing to God.

Good—To be pleasing in God's eyes. This word denotes a "stand alone" goodness. Another word translates to be "good, valuable, or virtuous for appearance or use." This type of good is not attained by ability or achievement, but is intrinsic in the character of the wife.

Becometh holiness—Reverent, beautifully separated to God. As the husband is to put the Lord first in all things, so is the wife. All else will be right when holiness is right.

False accusers—To falsely accuse or slander. The root word is the word for the devil. His name means slander, and Revelation 12:10 describes Satan as the accuser of the brethren.

🌴 The "Adorning" of Godly Character 🌴

"While they behold your chaste conversation coupled with fear. Whose adorning let it not be that outward adorning of plaiting the hair, and of wearing of gold, or of putting on of apparel; But let it be the hidden man of the heart, in that which is not corruptible, even the

ornament of a meek and quiet spirit, which is in the sight of God of great price" (I Peter 3:2-4). Adorning means decorating or drawing attention to. It seems to be something that you can do. What we can do, God will not do for us.

Heart—Thoughts, feelings, and Godly desires.

Meek—A gentle, mild, and humble attitude.

Quiet—A not easily disturbed, tranquil, peaceful and smooth attitude.

Corruptible—Decaying, temporary, mortal. A "not corruptible" heart can only come from an incorruptible Savior.

Great price—Expensive, valuable, of high cost. One other word defines "great price"—the word precious.

Think of it, wife, you have the opportunity to be precious in the sight of God. What a marvelous thought! What a wonderful privilege, to be a wife of pleasing character.

Photo:

Travis and Earlene Harris and children are missionaries to Lommel, Belgium.

Part Three

Biblical Principles for Blessings In the Christian Home

The rain descended...
And the winds blew
And beat upon the house;
And if fell not:
For it was founded upon a rock.
Matthew 7:25

12

The Christian Home
A Place Where We Desire
God's Blessings

"*Then Jesus went thence, and departed into the coasts of Tyre and Sidon. And, behold, a woman of Canaan came out of the same coasts, and cried unto him, saying, Have mercy on me, O Lord, thou son of David; my daughter is grievously vexed with a devil. But he answered her not a word.*

And his disciples came and besought him, saying, Send her away; for she crieth after us.

But he answered and said, I am not sent but unto the lost sheep of the house of Israel.

Then came she and worshipped him, saying, Lord, help me.

But he answered and said, It is not meet to take the children's bread, and to cast it to dogs.

And she said, Truth, Lord: yet the dogs eat of the crumbs which fall from their masters' table.

Then Jesus answered and said unto her, O woman, great is thy faith: be it unto thee even as thou wilt. And her daughter was made whole from that very hour" (Matthew 15:21-28).

The book of Matthew tells the story of the Syrophoenician woman, a Greek from Syrophoenicia.

She had a daughter that had a severe disease of some sort. She was *"grievously vexed with a devil."* No doubt this mother had been to others with the problem. No doubt this was a very dark and troubling time for her home. She, like we, had a problem that would require the help of the Lord.

She was a determined woman. She was very troubled about her daughter's condition, and was determined to receive the blessing of healing for her daughter. She was determined to seek out Christ. She was determined enough to go to Him, to cry out, to beg for her daughter's life. She made a spectacle of herself. The disciples were insensitive to her request. Jesus was in the transition ministry to the house of Israel. But she was determined in her cry. She desperately wanted a blessing from the Lord—and she got it!

"And Jacob was left alone; and there wrestled a man with him until the breaking of the day. And when he saw that he prevailed not against him, he touched the hollow of his thigh; and the hollow of Jacob's thigh was out of joint, as he wrestled with him. And he said, Let me go, for the day breaketh.

And he said, I will not let thee go, except thou bless me.

And he said unto him, What is thy name?

And he said, Jacob.

And he said, Thy name shall be called no more Jacob, but Israel: for as a prince hast thou power with God and with men, and hast prevailed.

And Jacob asked him, and said, Tell me, I pray thee, thy name.

And he said, Wherefore is it that thou dost ask after my name? And he blessed him there" (Genesis 32:24-29).

It was a dark and lonely night when Jacob began to wrestle with the Lord at Jabbok (Genesis 32:24). Jacob was on the run from Laban, his father-in-law. He was facing the wrath of Esau for 20-year-old sins that he had committed. His home was divided and in danger.

Jacob was wounded in the conflict. As the dawn

approached, the angel cried out; he begged to be let go. But Jacob's desire for blessing was too strong for him to release the pleading angel.

Jacob cried out, *"I will not let thee go, except thou bless me"* (Genesis 22:26). Jacob was a broken, weak, wounded man. But he was desperate for the work of God in his life and home. He was determined, un-yielding, bent upon receiving a blessing—and he got it!

Are we just as determined to want God's blessings upon our homes? Are we willing to lose sleep, to cry, to wrestle in prayer for the blessings of God upon our homes? Are we ardent in prayer, "begging" God for blessings upon our marriages and children? Is our prayer life for our family and home a casual thing? Is prayer for our home and children something that we do only in crisis situations?

I can think of no place closer to our hearts where we would want God's blessings than in our homes. **The blessings of God are accessed by prayer**. We, as the children of God, certainly have the privilege of prayer. Pray fervently for God's blessings upon your home—you can receive them!

🌴 Examples Of Blessings Upon The Home 🌴

The Women Who Brought Their Babies and Children to Jesus.

"And they brought young children to him that he should touch them: and his disciples rebuked those that brought them" (Mark 10:13). Mothers came bringing their children to Jesus, confident that Jesus would receive and bless them. It was not He who would turn them away, but the disciples, who probably wished to save the Master time and inconvenience. *"But when Jesus saw it, he was much displeased, and said unto them, Suffer the little children to come unto me, and forbid them not: for of such is the kingdom of God. And*

*he took them up in his arms, put his hands upon them,
and blessed them"* (Mark 10:16).

Rahab secured the blessing of God upon her home.

The book of Joshua tells the story of Rahab, the
harlot of Jericho, who harbored the Israelite spies
Joshua sent to see the city. When their presence was
known, Rahab hid the two spies under bundles of flax
upon her roof. Before letting them safely down the
outside wall, Rahab asked the spies for protection for
her family when Jericho fell. *"Now therefore, I pray you,
swear unto me by the LORD, since I have shewed you
kindness, that ye will also shew kindness unto my
father's house, and give me a true token"* (Joshua 2:1-12).

She based it all upon her faith in God. *"By faith the
harlot Rahab perished not with them that believed not,
when she had received the spies with peace"* (Hebrews
11:31).

The Shunammite woman brought a blessing upon her home.

The woman of Shunem, a great woman, showed
kindness to the man of God. *"And it fell on a day, that
Elisha passed to Shunem, where was a great woman; and
she constrained him to eat bread. And so it was, that as oft
as he passed by, he turned in thither to eat bread. And she
said unto her husband, Behold now, I perceive that this is
an holy man of God, which passeth by us continually. Let
us make a little chamber, I pray thee, on the wall; and let
us set for him there a bed, and a table, and a stool, and a
candlestick: and it shall be, when he cometh to us, that he
shall turn in thither. And it fell on a day, that he came
thither, and he turned into the chamber, and lay there.
And he said to Gehazi his servant, Call this Shunammite.
And when he had called her, she stood before him. And he
said unto him, Say now unto her, Behold, thou hast been
careful for us with all this care; what is to be done for
thee?"* (II Kings 4:8-13).

The one thing her heart desired, the one most important thing she did not have, was a child. Her husband was very old, and her hope for a son had long ago perished. But her kindness to the man of God brought this blessing to her home. Elisha said, *"About this season, according to the time of life, thou shalt embrace a son. And she said, Nay, my lord, thou man of God, do not lie unto thine handmaid. And the woman conceived, and bare a son at that season that Elisha had said unto her, according to the time of life"* (II Kings 4:8-17).

There is a spiritual principle in the story of Rahab and the Shunammite woman that can be applied in our homes. What is it? It is that as we give ourselves to the service of the Lord, as we obey Him, our prayers for His blessings are answered. *"Delight thyself also in the LORD; and he shall give thee the desires of thine heart"* (Psalm 37:4).

🌴 Homes Upon The Rock 🌴

A home that stands in testing times depends upon the hearing and obedience to the Word of God. *"Therefore whosoever heareth these sayings of mine, and doeth them, I will liken him unto a wise man, which built his house upon a rock: and the rain descended, and the floods came, and the winds blew, and beat upon that house; and it fell not: for it was founded upon a rock"* (Matthew 7:24-25).

The surefire method for not receiving God's blessings upon your home is to leave off obedience to the Word of God. *"And every one that heareth these sayings of mine, and doeth them not, shall be likened unto a foolish man, which built his house upon the sand: And the rain descended, and the floods came, and the winds blew, and beat upon that house; and it fell: and great was the fall of it"* (Matthew 7:26-27).

If our personal lives will be blessed because of being built upon the wisdom of God's Word, it stands to reason that our homes will be also.

1 3

A Place of Compassion and Forgiveness

"*For if ye forgive men their trespasses, your heavenly Father will also forgive you: But if ye forgive not men their trespasses, neither will your Father forgive your trespasses*" (Matthew 6:14-15).

"*And when ye stand praying, forgive, if ye have ought against any: that your Father also which is in heaven may forgive you your trespasses. But if ye do not forgive, neither will your Father which is in heaven forgive your trespasses*" (Mark 11:25-26).

"*And forgive us our sins; for we also forgive every one that is indebted to us. And lead us not into temptation; but deliver us from evil*" (Luke 11:4).

"*Take heed to yourselves: If thy brother trespass against thee, rebuke him; and if he repent, forgive him. And if he trespass against thee seven times in a day, and seven times in a day turn again to thee, saying, I repent; thou shalt forgive him*" (Luke 17:3-4).

Jesus Christ had much to say about forgiveness. He set the supreme example of forgiveness on the cross of Calvary as He cried, "*Father, forgive them; for they know not what they do.*" Because of His sacrifice, we have a place of forgiveness in Christ Jesus.

Unforgiveness is a burden that no one can live with for long. Unforgiveness has never been God's will or way.

Satan comes against us with accusations and condemnation. God warns, convicts, even chastises us for sin so that we may be reconciled to Him. He never leaves us in the condemnation, guilt, and hopelessness of our sins. What a blessing it is to have the assurance of God's compassion and forgiveness!

The Bible is clear that we also are to exercise these characteristics in our relationships with others. This is particularly applicable in our homes, as seen in Jesus' example of the forgiveness of the Father:

"A certain man had two sons: And the younger of them said to his father, Father, give me the portion of goods that falleth to me. And he divided unto them his living.

"And not many days after the younger son gathered all together, and took his journey into a far country, and there wasted his substance with riotous living. And when he had spent all, there arose a mighty famine in that land; and he began to be in want. And he went and joined himself to a citizen of that country; and he sent him into his fields to feed swine. And when he came to himself, he said, How many hired servants of my father's have bread enough and to spare, and I perish with hunger! I will arise and go to my father, and will say unto him, Father, I have sinned against heaven, and before thee, and am no more worthy to be called thy son: make me as one of thy hired servants. And he arose, and came to his father.

"But when he was yet a great way off, his father saw him, and had compassion, and ran, and fell on his neck, and kissed him.

"And the son said unto him, Father, I have sinned against heaven, and in thy sight, and am no more worthy to be called thy son.

"But the father said to his servants, Bring forth the best robe, and put it on him; and put a ring on his hand, and shoes on his feet: And bring hither the fatted calf, and kill it; and let us eat, and be merry: For this my son was dead, and is alive again; he was lost, and is found" (Luke 15:11-24).

Luke 15:11-19 demonstrates the drastic mistakes of sin. We see the son in his desire for the father's goods, in his departure to the far country, in his destitution in the famine, and finally in his desperation of soul at the hog pen. Many of us have made these same mistakes and have experienced the condemnation of soul that always is the result of sin. The devil would like to keep us right there, disabled as a casualty of spiritual warfare.

Luke 15:20-24 shows us the heart of our Father. While sin ravaged the son, this father was grieved. While he was away, the father waited and watched. When he turned toward home, the father was compassionate and delighted. There was no lingering condemnation, no reminders of past transgression. This son found complete forgiveness. He was restored to complete freedom and authority, and again enjoyed complete fellowship. What a wonderful picture this is of our own sinful nature and of God's great compassion and forgiveness.

We all live in "clay vessels." As such, we all are prone to mistakes and failures. The Bible admonishes, *"Wherefore let him that thinketh he standeth take heed lest he fall"* (I Corinthians 10:12). The Christian in the Christian home is no exception. We are vulnerable to the failures of our flesh.

Prince Bismarck of Prussia, statesman and architect of German unification in the 19th century, was once asked by Count Enzenburg to write something in his album. The page on which he was to write contained the autographs of Guizot and Thiers, French statesmen and historians. Guizot had written, "I have learned in my long life two rules of prudence. The first is to forgive much, the second is never to forget." Under this Thiers had written, "A little forgetting would not detract from the forgiveness." Bismarck added, "As for me, I have learned to forget much and ask to be forgiven much" (from *Youth Time With God*).

Bismarck's advice is solid for all of us and is especially valid in the Christian home. Sometimes, listening to the advice and description of the home by Christian psychologists and others, we get the idea that the Christian home is a Shangri-la, a place of dreamlike bliss and sticky sentiment where things are never wrong. More likely it is a place where our failures are evident, a place of no cover-up, for those in the home are those that know us best.

The Bible principle is simply forgiveness. First, remember that God is faithful to forgive our sins. *"If we confess our sins, he is faithful and just to forgive us our sins, and to cleanse us from all unrighteousness"* (I John 1:9). Upon the basis of God's forgiveness to us, we are to forgive others. *"And be ye kind one to another, tenderhearted, forgiving one another, even as God for Christ's sake hath forgiven you"* (Ephesians 4:32). Peter asked the question that is relevant in our dealings with others' offenses toward us when he said, *"Lord, how oft shall my brother sin against me, and I forgive him? till seven times?"* We have all wondered just how far we are expected to go at some time in our lives, haven't we? Jesus answered the question in Matthew 18:22, *"Jesus saith unto him, I say not unto thee, Until seven times: but, Until seventy times seven."* As He continually forgives us, we are to forgive others also.

Each of us needs a place of forgiveness and understanding. Every child should recognize his home as a place where he can find forgiveness and understanding when he has made youthful mistakes, improprieties, and yes, even fallen into sin. Certainly, these things must be dealt with and corrected in children. But when the discipline is over, there needs to be clear-cut forgiveness and forgetting. This will mean no rehashing of the same mistakes in future conversations.

The motivation toward forgiveness is compassion. The definition of compassion is "to preserve moderation in the passions, especially in anger or grief; hence of one who is not unduly disturbed by the errors, faults, sins of others, but bears them gently." *"Who can have compassion on the ignorant, and on them that are out of the way; for that he himself also is compassed with infirmity"* (Hebrews 5:2).

The application of the principle of forgiveness based upon this verse is especially poignant when addressed to the "over-reaction" among some parents when they discover a fault, problem, or sin in the lives of their children. (I must confess my own guilt in this.) Bearing "gently" with the "ignorant" and applying God's wisdom, which includes compassion and forgiveness, instead of "flying off the handle," is the Bible way of exacting godly behavior from our children.

A common problem among parents is a failure to recognize personal failures. There is also a tendency to rehearse old mistakes and failures of the past. Our children need the same things that we do. They need to know that they can be forgiven. They also need to believe that the old issues will be forgotten.

Your reaction, whether of anger or of forgiveness, displays your relationship with your Father. Remember that, *"God for Christ's sake hath forgiven you."* Let your compassion determine your reaction. Forgive completely and to complete restoration. God will bless us as we conform to His precept.

But as for me and my house,
we will serve the LORD.
Joshua 24:15

Aaron and Stacy Hoot and their children are
missionaries in Barahona, Dominican Republic. The
Hoot family now includes nine children (eight are
shown in the photo).

1 4

A Place to Prove the
Skeptics Wrong

"And again he entered into Capernaum after some days; and it was noised that he was in the house. And straightway many were gathered together, insomuch that there was not room to receive them, no, not so much as about the door: and he preached the word unto them. And they come unto him, bringing one sick of the palsy, which was borne of four. And when they could not come nigh unto him for the press, they uncovered the roof where he was: and when they had broken it up, they let down the bed wherein the sick of the palsy lay.

When Jesus saw their faith, he said unto the sick of the palsy, Son, thy sins be forgiven thee.

But there were certain of the scribes sitting there, and reasoning in their hearts, Why doth this man thus speak blasphemies? Who can forgive sins but God only?

And immediately when Jesus perceived in his spirit that they so reasoned within themselves, he said unto them, Why reason ye these things in your hearts? Whether is it easier to say to the sick of the palsy, Thy sins be forgiven thee; or to say, Arise, and take up thy bed, and walk? But that ye may know that the Son of man hath power on earth to forgive sins, (he saith to the sick of the palsy,) I say unto thee, Arise, and take up thy bed, and go thy way into thine house.

And immediately he arose, took up the bed, and went forth before them all; insomuch that they were all amazed, and glorified God, saying, We never saw it on this fashion" (Mark 2:1-12).

The Bible says in Mark 2:1 that "it was noised that Jesus was in the house." There can be no Christian home unless Jesus is in the home.

The *Baptist Challenge* tells the story of one little girl who often ate at her friends house next door. When they sat down to dinner, the family would take turns thanking the Lord for their food. After some months of coming for meals from time to time, the mother asked their visitor if she would like to pray. The little girl insisted that she did not know how. "Don't you pray at your house?" asked the mother. "No," answered the girl. "God does not live at our house like He does at yours."

Does God live at your house?

Not only was Jesus in the house, those in need were in the house. Through the means of four friends, a man sick with palsy was brought before Jesus as he preached the Word in the house. His need was met because of the presence of Jesus. It is always so. Many of us needlessly suffer and are troubled in our homes and lives because we will not allow Jesus to meet the need.

Jesus was in the house, the Word was preached in the house, the needy were in the house, but the skeptics were also in the house. They were lacking in faith. Mark 2:6 says they were *"reasoning in their hearts."* They were listening to their own counsel instead of the preached Word. They reasoned from worldly knowledge and philosophies of men rather than hearts of faith. They questioned the authority of the Son of God instead of embracing Him as Savior and Lord. We need to search our own hearts and the attitudes of our homes. We must guard against skepticism.

Our faith is constantly under attack outside the four walls of our homes and churches. God has given these to us as places of refuge and strengthening. The home and the church must prove the skeptics wrong. Endeavoring to fight against this constant onslaught means having our homes wed to Biblical principles for living instead of the world's wrong philosophies and priorities. It means looking for Jesus' presence and power in our midst, keeping ourselves in fellowship with Him.

If the church and the home fail to prove the skeptics wrong, who will? Does God live at your house?

🌴 The Skeptics 🌴

The Pharisees were bent on separation from all contact with sinners. Sadly, this blinded them to spiritual truths which God wants us to use in our daily lives. Jesus proved these skeptics wrong by showing them that God is concerned with forgiving sinners.

Jesus proved His deity to skeptics after His resurrection. *"To whom also he shewed himself alive after his passion by many infallible proofs, being seen of them forty days, and speaking of the things pertaining to the kingdom of God"* (Acts 1:3).

Peter said there would be many skeptics in these last days. *"Knowing this first, that there shall come in the last days scoffers, walking after their own lusts"* (II Peter 3:3). He noted for us that many skeptics are *"willingly ignorant"* (II Peter 3:5). As such, they will not listen to reason of Truth. They must be proven wrong.

🌴 Home Improvement 🌴

Can you say that the walls of your home reflect love for God? If so, how? Joshua made a positive declaration of love and service to the Lord. *"And if it seem evil unto you to serve the LORD, choose you this day whom ye will serve; whether the gods which your fathers served that were on the other side of the flood, or the gods of the Amorites, in whose land ye dwell: but as for me and my house, we will serve the LORD"* (Joshua 24:15). Has your family made a similar declaration? You need a definitive declaration of intention for your home.

God instructs us that His Word must have a place of preeminence in our homes. *"And these words, which I command thee this day, shall be in thine heart: and thou shalt teach them diligently unto thy children, and shalt talk of them when thou sittest in thine house, and when thou walkest by the way, and when thou liest down, and when thou risest up. And thou shalt bind them for a sign upon thine hand, and they shall be as frontlets between thine eyes. And thou shalt write them upon the posts of thy house, and on thy gates"* (Deuteronomy 6:6-9).

- Implanting of His Word, vs. 6
- Instruction of His Word, vs. 7
- Institution of His Word, vs. 7
- Indication of His Word, vs. 8
- Instilling of His Word, vs. 9

The overriding principle that we are to teach our children is *"the fear of the Lord"* (Psalm 34:11). Help them to know that His presence is real in homes and lives. You will teach this by attitude and action. It must be taught in the church and in the home.

15

Parental Responsibility and Leadership

"Train up a child in the way he should go: and when he is old, he will not depart from it" (Proverbs 22:6).

Who is responsible for a child gone bad? Who is responsible for the ultimate success or failure in the spiritual lives of our young people? I believe there are three areas of responsibility that are equally important and necessary for Proverbs 22:6 to be a valid principle of the Word of God.

Ecclesiastical responsibility is that which the church is accountable for. This would include but is not limited to: preaching the truth about salvation, presenting the facts about sin, and providing opportunities for service. Because of this portion of the training up of a child, it is imperative that the parents be in the will of God as they choose a church. There must also be loyalty and faithfulness to attendance and adherence to the church.

There is also **personal responsibility**, which is validated by much Scripture and exemplified by children who come from the same home and background, but go in opposite moral directions. Each individual is ultimately responsible for his own choices and actions. Of course, it is much easier for psychologists and parents to blame one another or the church for the children's actions than it is to accept the fact that their children are following the dictates of their own wicked hearts. I will address these issues further in a later chapter.

There is a third area of responsibility. In keeping with the theme of this book, I want to address the area of parental responsibility. While the church does have certain responsibilities in regard to preparing young people for the hostile environment they will experience in the world, it is not the church's responsibility alone. The burden is placed squarely and primarily upon the shoulders of parents in the Christian home. The church is the aid to the home in all of this. The real key is the church and the home working together to raise up the children.

🌲 The Parental Responsibility 🌲

Put Forth a Good Example, Consistently

Herein lies much of the problem when it comes to a child gone wrong. What they see and hear at home is not consistent. What is right and wrong is always changing, depending upon the mood and the frame of mind of the parents. Also, what they see and hear at home is not consistent with what they are taught at church. Consistency in the home is so important. It is amazing how children and teens will pick up on any little inconsistency.

Young people need a consistent example. They need to be taught that what is right is right and what is wrong is wrong, regardless of when and where it is. What they are taught at church about separation and Godliness needs to be reinforced at home. What they are taught about dating and about their relationships to the world and those in the world needs to be reinforced at home. What they are taught about priorities needs to be reinforced at home. It is no wonder that kids go bad when they hear one thing at church, only to hear and see something totally opposite at home. Why should they have any confidence in what they have been taught at church, if Mom and Dad don't?

Consider Deuteronomy 6:3-9, especially verses 5-7: *"And thou shalt love the LORD thy God with all thine heart, and with all thy soul, and with all thy might. And these words, which I command thee this day, shall be in thine heart: And thou shalt teach them diligently unto thy children, and shalt talk of them when thou sittest in thine house, and when thou walkest by the way, and when thou liest down, and when thou risest up."* Only after parents have met these requirements are they spiritually qualified to teach them to their children. Even then, they are to do it diligently, not halfheartedly, not occasionally, not just the week after revival. We cannot teach effectively what we do not practice consistently!

Dr. Harry Ironside well said, "The tree follows the bent of its early years, and so with our children. If taught to love the world and crave its fashions and follies in childhood, they are almost certain to live for the world when they come to mature years.

"On the other hand, if properly instructed as to the vanity of all that men of this present evil age live for from the beginning, they are in little danger of reversing that judgment as they grow older. Parents need to remember that it is not enough to tell their little ones of Jesus, or to warn them of the ways of the world. But they must see to it that, in their own lives, they exemplify their instruction. This will count above all else in the training of the young.

"To speak piously of separation to Christ while manifesting the spirit of the world in dress, the arrangement of the home, the company sought and kept, will readily be set down by observing little ones as dissimulation and hypocrisy. We need not wonder, then, if they grow up to cast all our words behind them, and to love what our ways proclaimed to be the real object of our hearts.

"Where a holy, cheerful atmosphere pervades the home, and Godly admonition is coupled with Godly living, parents can count on the Lord to keep their households following the right way." [1]

Promote the Program, Enthusiastically!

Participation shouldn't be optional. Participation in all church activities should be mandatory. When a young person misses a Sunday School class, choir rehearsal, a youth function, or other activity, whether by his own choice or the choice of his parents, he is the loser.

While a parent would not think of allowing the child to decide whether he will participate in school activities and in many cases, other activities (sports, drill teams, etc.), they readily allow their child the option in church activities. Be honest; which is more important? For which will we give answer to the Lord? I have never understood the logic behind punishing a child by not letting them attend a youth activity. The way to punish wrong behavior is not by keeping them away from godly influences.

The parent needs to recognize that the rearing of a child is a heart matter. The key to success is the keeping of the heart of the child. Any and all influences that assist in that effort make a parent's likelihood of success greater. The church is also charged with affecting the heart of every child and adult in its realm of influence. The more exposure the child has to any teaching or ministry of the church, the greater the assistance to the parent and the greater benefit to the child.

Promotion Should Be Oral

When it comes to supporting the program of the church enthusiastically, parents need to watch what they say in front of their children. Some parents talk about everything and everybody at home in front of their children. Then they wonder why their kids aren't enthusiastic about the church. We cannot help but be a

---

1 H. A. Ironside, *Notes on Proverbs*, Loizeaux Brothers, Neptune, 1975.

product of what we hear. Our children should not hear anything but positive words come out of our mouths when it comes to the church and the church members. This is especially true concerning those members who are responsible for ministering to the young people. There is no perfect situation or person. There will always be problems when it comes to interaction in the family. We may need to deal with a problem. But we should never involve our children in the problem.

Pray for the Lord's Wisdom, Regularly

Supernatural assistance is essential. The older your children get and the more complex the issues of life become, the more essential prayer is. To be a successful parent in this complex and changing society will only be accomplished with God's help. Each parent should realize that he does not have all the answers, nor does God expect him to. Christian parents, however, know One who does. We are admonished by James: *"If any of you lack wisdom, let him ask of God, that giveth to all men liberally, and upbraideth not; and it shall be given him"* (James 1:5).

Separation from Tradition is Needed

This statement may border on heresy in the eyes of some, but it may not be wise to base everything we do regarding our children on what our parents did. Who's to say that our parents were right all of the time? Who's to say our parents didn't make some mistakes here and there? Certainly we should weigh their example, counsel, and advice carefully. Certainly we should "search for the old paths." But there is only one real source of wisdom—the Word of God. It will take the leadership of the Holy Spirit to help us to discern it. Our only weapon against the wiles of Satan is spiritual discernment and Biblical enlightenment. Now more than ever as Christian parents, we need a real spirit of discernment.

*Train up a child in the way
he should go: and when he is old,
he will not depart from it.*
Proverbs 22:6

*Pictured are Deborah Roy, daughter of Adam
and Janet Roy, and Stephen Stewart, son of
Charles and Suzanne Stewart. Deborah and
Stephen are part of the growing heritage of
Bayou Drive Baptist Church.*

16

The Child's Responsibility

"Train up a child in the way he should go: and when he is old, he will not depart from it" (Proverbs 22:6).

Who is to blame for a child gone bad? Who is responsible for the ultimate success or failure in the spiritual lives of our young people? The answer to that question may lie in your view of Proverbs 22:6. Was this verse a promise, or a principle of the Word of God?

If Proverbs 22:6 is a promise, meaning that it is true 100% of the time, then it appears that the parents and the church are to blame for a child gone bad. Both the home and the church have certain responsibilities, as we have already seen, in teaching and training children. So if the verse is a promise, then somewhere there was a breakdown in the training process.

But if Proverbs 22:6 is a promise, how do you explain this common occurrence? Two children are raised in the same home, raised under the sound of the same gospel, raised with the same Biblical principles and convictions, raised with the same parental examples, yet they go in opposite directions regarding the things of the Lord.

I believe that Proverbs 22:6 is set forth as a principle, not a promise. This means that if the principles of child rearing set forth in the Scriptures are followed, the child will most likely live by these principles all of his or her life. This is not a cop-out for bad parents or poor church training. This view, in my opinion, allows children to be ultimately responsible for their own actions.

When God created man, He created him with the ability to choose. That is apparent from the story of Adam and Eve in Genesis chapters 1-3. After they were instructed how they were to live, they deliberately chose to disobey. Children are ultimately responsible for their own spiritual success or failure. The church and the home can equip them, instruct them, prepare them, and provide the tools needed to succeed. But ultimately it is up to each child to decide what choices they will make.

🌴 The Child's Responsibility Concerning Salvation 🌴

Preached Truth Must Become Accepted Truth.

The church's responsibility is to preach the truth. The parents' responsibility is to teach the truth. As discussed already, this teaching is done by both precepts and lifestyle. I don't believe we could over-emphasize the need for a Godly parental example in the home. Consistent living is the best preaching your children will ever hear.

It is the personal responsibility of every child or adult to accept or reject the truth. Ultimately all Biblical truth must be accepted or rejected on a personal basis.

Power for changed lives comes through salvation. Conforming to the rules is not salvation. Sometimes "good" children grow up, go away, and never return to their Biblical foundation because they were never saved in the first place. Conversion is the result of salvation. These children had never been converted; they had only conformed to the rules and regulations set down by those in authority.

Personal Choice is Essential for Salvation.

"He that believeth on him is not condemned: but he that believeth not is condemned already, because he hath not believed in the name of the only begotten Son of God" (John 3:18).

🌴 The Child's Responsibility Concerning Sin 🌴

Sin is a Choice

Our children sin because they want to. Our children sin because they willfully disregard the warnings that go forth from the pulpit. Our children sin because they disregard the teachings and pattern of their parents.

When we understand the awful consequence of sin, the wreck and ruin, the destruction and havoc of sin, we will be more careful in our approach to our own responsibility.

Sin's Results are the Result of Individual Choices

Every young person earns by his own choices his reputation, rebellion, and resentment. The results must rest upon the individual.

Parents tend to take the rap and bear the guilt. Sometimes the church is blamed. These individuals earn their own results by their own actions and acquaintances, just as each of us do.

🌴 The Child's Responsibility Concerning Service 🌴

Service Requires Priority Choices

When we say we do not have time to serve, we really say it's just not a priority for us. Every person is blessed with the same amount of time. What we do with our time is ultimately our own choice.

Teaching, both at home and by the church, provides the tools to know how to set proper priorities. But priorities are set by individual choice. *"Then said Jesus unto his disciples, If any man will come after me, let him deny himself, and take up his cross, and follow me"* (Matthew 16:24).

Lo, children are a heritage of the LORD: and the fruit of the womb is his reward.
Psalm 127:3

Derrick and Nadine Dacas and their children Debra, Scott and Samuel, are missionaries to Kingston, Jamaica.

A Place of Discipline

Without a doubt, the most controversial subject when it comes to child rearing is discipline. Many parents have been convinced by the "experts" that to actually strike a child is barbaric. They contend that we have advanced beyond that point and should resort to a more modern form of discipline, if we discipline at all. They suggest a form of discipline that is more socially acceptable, one that is not likely to warp the child's self image. We also hear horror stories regarding discipline and the government social services' intervention in child-rearing in the home. But regardless of the "expert's" advice or the opinions of government watchdogs, God's Word is still the supreme authority in all matters. This includes the discipline and correction of children.

🌲 The Misconceptions 🌲

Due to cultural changes, "scientific research," and parenting "experts," many parents, including Christian parents, have developed non-Biblical views regarding child discipline (spanking). Those parents who do follow the Biblical mandate to discipline are made to feel guilty, and they become hesitant about their responsibility. The book of Proverbs warns against instruction that is contrary to the Word of God. *"Cease, my son, to hear the instruction that causeth to err from the words of knowledge"* (Proverbs 19:27).

Misconception #1

The philosophies taught by the modern gurus of child behavior are based upon absolute truth.

The truth is that these philosophies are constantly changing. Those who base the discipline of their children upon the "expert's" voice find their methods changing often. The more advanced the experts become in their knowledge of human behavior, the more changes they make regarding the do's and don'ts of child discipline. Why not rely upon the words and wisdom of the One who created man in the first place? Who could have more knowledge of human behavior than the Creator?

As the Creator, God was fully aware of the behavioral problems that would exist in His creation. He provided us with the most authoritative Book ever written on the subject. In His Word, the Lord is very specific in regard to the discipline of our children. When parents begin to search for answers regarding child discipline, the Bible is the place to look. Only in the Scriptures will they find the absolute truth regarding this very important subject. *"Forever, O LORD, thy word is settled in heaven"* (Psalm 119:89).

Misconception #2

Children are inherently good and therefore they do not need to be spanked. Rather, they need only to be put in the correct environment.

The basis for almost all the anti-spanking teaching is humanism. Humanism teaches, among other things, that man is inherently good and does not possess a sin nature. The truth is that we all have sinful natures that must be corrected and held in check.

"Behold, I was shapen in iniquity; and in sin did my mother conceive me" (Psalms 51:5).

"As it is written, there is none righteous, no, not one: ...For all have sinned, and come short of the glory of God" (Romans 3:10, 23).

"Wherefore, as by one man sin entered into the world, and death by sin; and so death passed upon all men, for that all have sinned" (Romans 5:12).

"The wicked are estranged from the womb: they go astray as soon as they be born, speaking lies" (Psalms 58:3).

Simply changing the environment of a child will not change the fact that he or she was born with a sin nature that is bent on sinning.

Misconception #3

Spanking causes a child to become violent.

If you are stopped for speeding and have to pay a fine of $100.00, are the police teaching you to be a spendthrift with your money? Are they teaching you to be wasteful? After you pay the fine, are you going to get this irresistible urge to start giving your money away? The answer of course is no. You are fined for speeding to get your attention and to restrain your behavior. The same principle applies to discipline. Biblical spanking is an act of love, designed to amend a child's behavior. *"The law of the wise is a fountain of life, to depart from the snares of death"* (Proverbs 13:14). *"Correct thy son, and he shall give thee rest; yea, he shall give delight unto thy soul"* (Proverbs 29:17).

As I said at the beginning of this chapter, this area of discipline is the most sensitive and controversial subject concerning child rearing. I realize that some of you may have preconceived ideas in this area. I ask you to maintain an open mind and heart and let the Lord do the teaching. The Christian home, as with all areas of Christian life, is one of constant learning and growth.

🌳 The Merit 🌳

While some parents would never think of deliberately disobeying the commands of the Scriptures, they do just that when they fail to practice Biblical discipline.

The Bible does more than condone spanking, it commands it. *"Withhold not correction from the child: for if thou beatest him with the rod, he shall not die"* (Proverbs 23:13). The bottom line is that parents who do not spank their children are unscriptural and are in direct disobedience to the Word. The Bible is very specific in the instruction. No one can successfully argue against the fact that God expects parents to use spanking as a form of discipline.

Spanking Expresses Love

"He that spareth his rod hateth his son: but he that loveth him chasteneth him betimes" (Proverbs 13:24).

It is not love, but rather lack of love that causes a parent to refrain from spanking. Love is primarily an action, not an emotion. Parents need to realize that spanking is not something they do *to* a child, but *for* a child. A parent who spanks is acting in love to meet his child's need. Contrary to modern philosophy, Biblical correction does not drive children away. Discipline, administered scripturally, will be an effective way of demonstrating the love of the parent for the child.

Spanking Expels Foolishness

"Foolishness is bound in the heart of a child; but the rod of correction shall drive it far from him" (Proverbs 22:15).

Discipline, administered properly, will correct the natural tendency to go astray. However, leaving children to themselves without any correction will result in much heartache. Take time to read the background behind I Samuel 3:13, II Samuel 13, and I Kings 1:5-6. You will see the results of a failure to discipline.

Spanking Helps To Escape Destruction

"Withhold not correction from the child: for if thou beatest him with the rod, he shall not die. Thou shalt beat him with the rod, and shalt deliver his soul from hell" (Proverbs 23:13-14).

Children are born with a natural tendency toward sin. *"The wicked are estranged from the womb: they go astray as soon as they be born, speaking lies"* (Psalm 58:3).

"Wherein in time past ye walked according to the course of this world, according to the prince of the power of the air, the spirit that now worketh in the children of disobedience: Among whom also we all had our conversation in times past in the lusts of our flesh, fulfilling the desires of the flesh and of the mind; and were by nature the children of wrath, even as others" (Ephesians 2:1-3).

Children do not have to be taught to sin. They sin naturally because it is their nature. We know, of course, that the end result of following the dictates of our sinful nature is destruction in a place called hell. It is the responsibility of the parents to guide their children away from destruction. Parents warn children of dangers in this life, i.e. don't talk to strangers, don't play in the street, etc. The warnings are made sternly and with enforcement to produce an effect. Solomon tells us in Proverbs 23:14 that spanking is an effective deterrent to destructive behavior.

Spanking Effects Wisdom

"The rod and reproof give wisdom: but a child left to himself bringeth his mother to shame" (Proverbs 29:15).

The object of child rearing is not to teach them to eat or dress properly, to learn to use good manners, or to get along with other children. The goal is not to raise a star athlete or a brilliant student. The goal of Christian parents should be to instill character in their children. Solomon uses the word *wisdom*. Wisdom is not knowledge; rather, it is the application of knowledge in real life situations. It is character. Right character will make the right choices. Spanking applied in a Biblical manner will mold lifelong character.

Spanking Ensures Rest

"Correct thy son, and he shall give thee rest; yea, he shall give delight unto thy soul" (Proverbs 29:17).

Many parents have been driven to an early grave because of a rebellious child! Nothing brings more pain to the heart of a parent than a child who is out of control. Read the story of Absalom in II Samuel 18, and hear the pain of David's heart, *"O my son Absalom, my son, my son Absalom! Would God I had died for thee, O Absalom, my son, my son!"* (II Samuel 18:33). Parents can do much to ensure that the days spent with their children are days filled with joy and happiness. Much needless pain and sorrow can be avoided simply by following the Word of God in regard to discipline.

Spanking Encourages Righteousness

"Now no chastening for the present seemeth to be joyous, but grievous: nevertheless afterward it yieldeth the peaceable fruit of righteousness unto them which are exercised thereby" (Hebrews 12:11).

The goal of all discipline ought to be to produce righteous living. That is the goal and pattern of our Heavenly Father for His children. This is the thrust of this passage of Scripture. God wants us to live righteously. When we do not, He chastises us to correct us and to bring about righteousness in our lives. This discipline or chastisement is never joyous for either parent or child. But, while it is not pleasant for either, the end result will be enjoyed by both.

Please notice that the rod referred to in the Bible is described as coming from the branch of a tree or the stem of a bush. The instrument used in spanking should be sufficient to cause pain but never injury. The spanking instrument is not a weapon; it is a tool to be used in the amending of a child's behavior.

I ask you to approach this counsel with a prayerful attitude and an open heart. The controversial nature of the subject will require the direction of the Lord for proper discernment. No one is an expert; all are students. We look to Him for teaching.

"Lo, children are an heritage of the LORD: and the fruit of the womb is his reward. As arrows are in the hand of a mighty man; so are children of the youth. Happy is the man that hath his quiver full of them: they shall not be ashamed, but they shall speak with the enemies in the gate" (Psalm 127:3-5).

Chastening...yieldeth the peaceable fruit of righteousness unto them which are exercised thereby.
Hebrews 12:11

Mr. and Mrs. Richard Weimer and their family are missionaries in Dresden, Germany. Missionary kids are often a major part of the worship service!

1 8

A Place of Discipline
Part 2

We have been looking into the most controversial subject in the Christian home, the subject of discipline. We have not discussed opinions about this subject, nor are we taking a vote. Rather, we are discussing discipline based upon the authority of the Word of God.

Under the title of "The Misconceptions" concerning child discipline, we have looked into the popular ideas of sociology and psychology. We found these ideas, for the most part, to stand in direct opposition to the Bible. Likewise, they ignore the common sense approach that has been proven by time. We have also looked at specific Bible references to explain the merits of disciplining children. As we studied the book of Proverbs in this light, it was amazing to see the various effects that are promised to conscientious parents.

The key to successful discipline is the manner in which it is delivered. Sheer brutality is very wrong and is opposed to the Spirit of God. There is a great difference between discipline and abuse. Nowhere in the Scriptures are parents given the right to abuse their child. Abuse fills the heart of the child with anger and only serves to alienate them from their parents. The "iron hand" must wear a "velvet glove," which is to say, that strict discipline must be administered in great love.

🌴 The Manner 🌴

Consider the following guidelines concerning discipline:

When possible, spanking should be done in private.

The purpose of spanking is not to humiliate the child but to teach right behavior. Remember to keep the communication line open between you and the child. When the discipline is over, you want your relationship to be one of unity with the child.

Begin early in spanking a child.

"Chasten thy son while there is hope, and let not thy soul spare for his crying" (Proverbs 19:18). *"He that spareth his rod hateth his son: but he that loveth him chasteneth him betimes"* (Proverbs 13:24).

The word *betimes* in Proverbs 13:24 means early. A general rule to follow is that when a child is old enough to understand the instruction and has the ability to comply, he or she then becomes fully accountable for his actions.

Proverbs 19:18 gives the same encouragement to begin applying Biblical correction early. *"Chasten thy son while there is hope, and let not thy soul spare for his crying."* This verse has the implication that there may come a time when it is too late to begin administering correction. Many parents have come to the realization that Biblical correction is needed in their little darling, only to find out that they waited too late to start. The discomfort which results from being spanked should always be far in excess of the pleasure enjoyed by doing wrong.

Too many times the correction only serves to make the child angry. He remembers the enjoyment of the wrongdoing. He promptly forgets the punishment. But he harbors resentment toward the parent who ineffectively administered it. The objective of the punishment is to build respect, not resentment. The child should understand that in the long run, he will always be the loser. The child should never be left thinking, "I know that I got a spanking, but it was worth it because I had a great time," "I got my way," etc. The punishment must deter the action.

A parent should state very clearly why a child is being spanked and provide some corrective instruction.

"The rod and reproof give wisdom..." (Proverbs 29:15).

Many well-meaning parents have been faithful in delivering the rod, only to leave their children wondering why they were disciplined. For all they know, Mom or Dad may have had a bad day and they just happened to be the recipients of their anger and frustration. *"And, ye fathers, provoke not your children to wrath: but bring them up in the nurture and admonition of the Lord."* (Ephesians 6:4). Notice the words *nurture* and *admonition*. The word nurture implies disciplinary action. Admonition deals with instruction. Biblical discipline of children must include a time of instruction.

Before spanking, a parent should ask the question, "What did you do?" This question establishes the factual basis for the spanking. Don't ask, "Why did you do it?" This will lead to a long list of excuses, given in order to justify the action and avert punishment. "Was that the right thing to do?" This question establishes guilt.

"What should you have done?" This question allows the parent insight to know that the child did know what he should have done. Or, if he didn't, it allows him to take corrective measures to insure that the same error is not repeated. "What will you do next time?" This question elicits from the child a commitment to do right in the future.

After administering the spanking, reaffirm your love to the child, state your willingness to forgive, then pray.

Ask God for wisdom, for peace to be established in your relationship with the child, for protection and guidance for the child.

Parents should always support each other in the discipline of the children.

Children will do anything they can to avoid a spanking. They will use any opportunity they can to divide Mom and Dad when it comes to discipline. Parents must present a united front when it comes to discipline, at all times. Parent, do not fall into the trap of being the "good guy" and allowing your partner to be the "bad guy" to your children. Your children should always understand that you fully support each other in this matter.

Parent, you have an awesome responsibility. You would do well to become very familiar with these Bible principles of discipline. If applied early, they will be of incalculable value to you and your child as he/she comes to maturity.

Unfortunately, there is only one perfect Father and that is our heavenly Father. He is the only parent who has never made a mistake in this area of discipline. Try as we might as parents to be perfect, it will never happen. We will always be prone to mistakes. Because of that, we need to be ready to admit when we are wrong and apologize at all times.

🌴 The Misapplication 🌴

Following is a list of some of the more common mistakes made by parents.

1. The spanking is only painful enough to be uncomfortable. It is not painful enough to outweigh the pleasure of the disobedience.

2. Offenses are dealt with inconsistently. An offense elicits a spanking one day and is ignored the next day. This leads to much confusion. If necessary, parents should publish a written set of guidelines along with the consequence if these guidelines are not followed. If nothing else, this will assure fair and consistent administration of discipline.

3. Standards of behavior are not clearly defined and understood. This is the result of insufficient time and effort on the parents' part to educate the child. As in all other human relationships, communication is the key.

4. Parents talk too much instead of acting. This is a result of lack of dedication to the task of rearing children in God's pattern.

5. The discipline handed down is out of proportion to the offense committed. This dilutes the effect of sterner measures when they are warranted.

6. The discipline is administered out of anger or frustration of the parent. Discipline should never be administered in anger. Take time to cool off before taking action.

7. Parents give up too soon. A strong-willed child must be dealt with in such a way that his or her will is effectively broken. This may involve repeated spankings. The parent must win all confrontations of the will.

One last note on this subject is in order. To leave a child to himself is to manifest a spirit of indifference as to the well-being of the child. To be unnecessarily severe in correcting him is to err in the other direction. To find a happy medium should be the desire of every parent. In all correction, a child should be made to realize that it is his good that is being sought. Never should a child be left in doubt as to the love of his parents.

Mom and Dad, we have an awesome responsibility given to us by God to be the guardians of the precious children that He sees fit to put into our care. We would do well to follow the teaching of our Heavenly Father in this area of discipline. Remember again the words of Solomon, *"Cease, my son, to hear the instruction that causeth to err from the words of knowledge"* (Proverbs 19:27).

For further information on the important area of discipline, read Deuteronomy 4:9, 6:6-7; Psalm 128; Ephesians 6:4; I Timothy 3:4.

I must be fit for a child to follow,
Scorning the places where loose men wallow;
Knowing how much he shall learn from me,
I must be fair as I'd have him be.
I must come home to him day by day,
Clean as the morning I went away.
I must be fit for a child's glad greeting;
His are eyes that there is no cheating.
He must behold me in every test,
Not at my worst but my very best;
He must be proud when my life is done
To have men know that he is my son.

—Edgar A. Guest

19

A Place of Father's Leadership

"And, ye fathers, provoke not your children to wrath: but bring them up in the nurture and admonition of the Lord" (Ephesians 6:4).

The Christian home is a place of many facets. One of the most important of these is the role of the father. This area cannot be over-emphasized. It is a sad fact that many homes today are led by single moms because of divorce. The church needs to take up the slack in this area by providing surrogate father figures for children in this situation. We want to focus on the role of the father in this chapter. We will not exhaust the subject, but it is a very needed discussion.

Parenting is a great responsibility. This is true of a mother, but even more so of the father. The Bible is full of examples of fathers that were failures. David pampered Absalom and set a bad example. The results were tragic. Eli failed to discipline his two sons. The results were disgrace of his name, disdain for the things of God, and defeat of his nation. Isaac spoiled Esau; Rebekah favored Jacob. The result was a divided home. Parental failure seems to have been the rule rather than the exception in the family histories recorded in the Bible. Rare indeed is the Abraham of whom God could say, *"For I know him, that he will command his children and his household after him, and they shall keep the way of the LORD"* (Genesis 18:19). But even Abraham had a rebellious son, Ishmael, who grew up to be a "wild man."

If we are serious in the endeavor to serve Christ, we must be serious about the Christian home. Dad, it will not just happen. It will require dedication, sacrifice, and effort on our part. The results, however, will be well worth it. The Bible is an unfailing source of guidance. Parent, I admonish you to give yourself to an intense study of such passages as Ephesians 5:15-6:4, Colossians 3:18-21, I Timothy 3:1-13, and I Peter 3:1-7. Father, a sincere study of these passages should bring every Christian man to a resolution to be the father that God intends us to be. I call this the "Resolution of the Christian Father." This resolution can only be kept as we receive the power of the indwelling Spirit of God.

The "Resolution of the Christian Father" can be broken down into three areas of commitment.

🌴 Live as a Father 🌴

The resolve is built upon the following verses: *"Be filled with the Spirit"* (Ephesians 5:18), and *"Let the word of Christ dwell in you richly in all wisdom"* (Colossians 3:16). No one can live as a father without being activated by the Spirit of God and dominated by the Word of God. It is impossible to be a husband or father without supernatural enablement. This is true of all areas of Christian living, of course, but is especially true in the most demanding roles of human relationships — fatherhood and motherhood. Your Christian living will come into closer scrutiny and require more honesty in your home than in any other arena of life.

The happiest days of living as a father are the reflection of an obedient walk with God in the light of His Word. This will come through the conscious awareness of the unquenched and ungrieved Spirit in his life. It is no accident that the above verses that command "filling of the Spirit" and the "dwelling of the Word in you" result in overflowing joy and happiness. Please note that the contexts of both of these Scriptures are set in living the Christian life in the home.

🌴 Love As A Father 🌴

God gives the command, *"Husbands, love your wives, even as Christ also loved the church, and gave himself for it"* (Ephesians 5:25). Since it is God's command, failure to obey it is sin. Such love can only be generated and governed by the indwelling and the infilling of the Spirit. This is love that gives and forgives, love that loves unto death, love that overflows to everyone in the home. Steadfast, unconditional love like this produces an answer to every evil force that threatens the joy, kindness, goodness, faithfulness, gentleness, and self-control of the home. *"But the fruit of the Spirit is love, joy, peace, longsuffering, gentleness, goodness, faith, meekness, temperance: against such there is no law"* (Galatians 5:22-23). One of the crying needs in most homes is the resolve of a father to submit to the Word of God and to sense the Spirit of God so that the love of God can be demonstrated in his home and among his children.

🌴 Lead As A Father 🌴

Look again at our text verse, *"And, ye fathers, provoke not your children to wrath: but bring them up in the nurture and admonition of the Lord"* (Ephesians 6:4). It is a divine demand made upon fathers that they lead. Paul is addressing a common failure of parents in this verse. That is the abuse of authority, breaking the spirit of the child and discouraging all aspirations and expectations. Leadership is not dictatorship—that is abuse.

The opposite of parental abuse of power and authority calls for three areas of leadership responsibility.

Caring Leadership

The Christian husband and father is to nurture both wife and children physically, mentally, and spiritually. The family must know that Dad cares. My own boys are grown and married, but they still expect a hug from Dad. Your children need to know that they can count on you to be there for them, even if they are grown. It is possible to be available without being accessible. You can be in the same room, but so engrossed in the paper, or television, or a hobby that you are inaccessible. The children are denied the touch of a hand, the listening ear, or a wrestling match on the floor.

You can also be available but not adaptable: "It's not the right time"; "I've got on the wrong clothes"; "I'm in a hurry." Caring leadership takes everything into account, then decides in the child's favor. Dr. Charles Stanley says, "Fathers spend more time watching a commercial four times a day than they do with their children all day (37 seconds)." That shouts to a child, "I am not worth anything to my daddy." Children need your acceptance and love.

Correcting Leadership

"Bring them up in the nurture and admonition of the Lord." This word *nurture* carries the idea of learning through discipline. It is translated *chastening* in Hebrews 12. *"He that loveth him chasteneth him betimes"* (Proverbs 13:24) says that a loving father is a chastening father. The discipline is to be administered with much love, with reason, and much prayer if it is to nurture. Modern psychology and philosophy scorn any form of discipline. What God says, however, supersedes what man says.

Counseling Leadership

"Bring them up in the nurture and admonition of the Lord." This takes in the whole sphere of instruction and inspiration. Much of this will be common sense advice and admonition, but even more importantly, it will be the teaching of God's Word at family altar, in regular conversation, and in those special sessions where the children let their hair down and talk. *"And these words, which I command thee this day, shall be in thine heart: And thou shalt teach them diligently unto thy children, and shalt talk of them when thou sittest in thine house, and when thou walkest by the way, and when thou liest down, and when thou risest up. And thou shalt bind them for a sign upon thine hand, and they shall be as frontlets between thine eyes. And thou shalt write them upon the posts of thy house, and on thy gates"* (Deuteronomy 6:6-9).

Father, find time for your children. Make sure they always know that you are available, attainable, and adaptable enough to find time for them and that no activity or acquaintance puts you out of their reach. Tuck them into bed when possible, and read and tell stories as often as you can. Take time to be a part of their activities. Be sure that mealtime is a family time in your home. Don't let the TV or busy schedules rob you of sitting down as a family at least once a day.

Make a special time for them. Give them a Saturday morning or an evening on a regular basis, not with a sports team or scout organization, but with *them*. It does not have to be elaborate or expensive. Make it a time together. Go someplace or do something they suggest. Give them your ear and make sure they know that you are available to listen to their problems, interests, and victories. Keep it simple, but make it their time with Dad.

Father, God has entrusted you with a great responsibility, but the rewards of being a father are innumerable. May I suggest that you write a "pledge of allegiance" to your family, then keep it to remind yourself of your great responsibility as a Dad.

🌲 A Father's Pledge 🌲

I pledge allegiance to my home—to my wife—to my sons and daughters. I will honor my home and consider the support of it as a sacred trust. I will do more than this. I will take time to cultivate friendship between my family and myself. I will not be too busy when they need me—even though it is only to catch a football or mend a broken doll. I will love my children as only I can. I will compliment their mother's hours of care and concern. I will introduce my children to Christ. I will exemplify Christ's standard before them and share with them the joys of Christian values in a Christian home.

The Father Heart of God

"But now, O LORD, thou art our father; we are the clay, and thou our potter; and we all are the work of thy hand" (Isaiah 64:8).

Most of us can remember making mud-pies. The earth is mixed with water to get it to just the right texture. The mud-cakes are fashioned as the mud yields to our pressure. This verse describes the child of God as *the clay* or "mud-cakes," with characteristics of pliability, submissiveness, and surrender.

God is the potter. He fashions the clay on the wheel—moving His hands, ever so gently, so as to make us according to His master plan. He has no rejects. Every piece of spiritual pottery He makes is perfect and fit for the Master's use. Our Heavenly Father fashions His children for their good and His glory.

He has entrusted fathers with the responsibility of leading, blending, molding, and finishing vessels for Him in our homes. Father, this is the most important work that you will do in this life. You cannot afford to fail in this task. We, as earthly fathers, ought to rear our children to our joy and their good. In order to do so, we will need help from God. We need to follow the supreme example of Fatherhood, the Lord Himself. We can see in His example that:

⚘ God Is A Loving Father ⚘

"Now our Lord Jesus Christ himself, and God, even our Father, which hath loved us..." (II Thessalonians 2:16). He loves His children. He moves all obstacles for His children. He knows His children need His love, and need to know that He loves them. Even so, our earthly children need love from their earthly fathers. They must know their father loves them if they are to enjoy life as God intended it to be. Somehow, Father, you must let your children know that you love them.

⚘ God is a Faithful Father ⚘

"Your heavenly Father will also forgive you" (Matthew 6:14).

"Yet your heavenly Father feedeth them. Are ye not much better than they?" (Matthew 6:32).

"For your heavenly Father knoweth that ye have need of all these things" (Matthew 6:32).

Our Heavenly Father is always there for us. He promised never to leave or forsake us. He is with us in the calm and peace, as well as the raging sea. Children need to know that their father will be there for them. The test of fatherhood is in the everyday, in the problems and in the good times.

⚘ God is a Forgiving Father ⚘

"And when ye stand praying, forgive, if ye have ought against any: that your Father also which is in heaven may forgive you your trespasses." Our Heavenly Father forgives our sins. He cleanses and remembers our sins no more. When He forgives us, we can rest in the assurance that our sins are gone forever. Dad, your children need to know that you will forgive them too. If you can't forgive, you need to ask God for the grace to

forgive your children. Forget the past and restore the relationship that is lacking.

🌴 God is a Longsuffering Father 🌴

"The LORD is merciful and gracious, slow to anger, and plenteous in mercy" (Psalm 103:8). Our Heavenly Father is longsuffering and patient with His children. He is waiting for us to repent and to come back to Him. Our children need a father who will give them time to grow, to fail, to repent, and to change. Father, be patient with your children. Allow them the time to return to a life of rightness and good standing.

🌴 God is a Compassionate Father 🌴

"For thou, Lord, art good, and ready to forgive; and plenteous in mercy unto all them that call upon thee" (Psalm 86:5). Our Heavenly Father is touched with the feeling of our infirmities. He is moved with compassion upon His children in their struggles and weaknesses. God looks upon His children with pity. Father, be compassionate toward your children. Of course, they have struggles and show weaknesses. They are made of the same clay that we are. They are in a battle with the world, their flesh, and the devil. Somehow, let them know compassion and pity in their times of difficulty.

As we review these characteristics of our Heavenly Father, this is my prayer:

"God, help us to be like you; loving, faithful, forgiving, longsuffering, and compassionate. Amen."

🌴 Remembering Dad 🌴

A laugh and a shout, a big "Yahoo"...
He surely was a Christian and preacher too,
But he was my Dad through and through.

He was tenderness, a tear, and godly fear,
Some called upon him from far and near,
But he was just Dad when he was here.

He preached with thunder and with fire;
Winning souls to Jesus was his great desire.
Dad's life was one a boy could admire.

Troubles and heartaches? He had plenty.
Family and church— problems were many,
But Dad had a heart that would reach to any.

Came that day, he suffered and died,
Of course we all wept and cried,
But Dad wouldn't have come back if we had tried.

Now his body lies beneath cold dark sod,
But he's not there—he's home with God.
Dad's prayer: "You come, too, when you get the nod."

So Dad, although you're a world away,
We love you still and wait the day,
When we come to you by God's Only Way.

By Wayne Hudson
In honor of Father, Harvey Hudson
June 13, 2001

21

A Place of Mother's Love

"Likewise, ye wives, be in subjection to your own husbands; that, if any obey not the word, they also may without the word be won by the conversation of the wives; while they behold your chaste conversation coupled with fear. Whose adorning let it not be that outward adorning of plaiting the hair, and of wearing of gold, or of putting on of apparel; But let it be the hidden man of the heart, in that which is not corruptible, even the ornament of a meek and quiet spirit, which is in the sight of God of great price" (I Peter 3:1-4).

In past chapters we have investigated the various responsibilities that are associated with the building of a Christian home and the blessings of being part of one. As with everything that is worthwhile, the Lord will bless those who will meet the conditions laid down in His Holy Word.

I want to begin to look at the responsibilities of the mother in the Christian home. Like the father, the mother has a very important place to fulfill if the home is to be a successful one. Many of the problems of society would be averted if we had a generation of mothers who were committed to Bible principles of motherhood.

The work of a mother is unending, demanding, and very diverse. The father of the home has the responsibility for setting the standards of the home and providing leadership in these. But most of the time, it is the mother that provides the administrative ability which puts those standards into practice in the home. She is the super-glue that holds everything together in the Christian home and the lubricant by which it all runs smoothly.

What are the tools that she must have in order to accomplish these things? At best, we can only skim the surface as we look at these in the next few articles. Of course, as the title suggests, the overriding quality that must be present is love. The next few chapters will examine four areas where love must be the dominant theme, but there are some prerequisites given in the book of I Peter that need to be investigated first.

I Peter 3 begins by looking at the example of Christ described in I Peter 2. He essentially says to every mother, "Follow the example of the Savior." He says the same thing to husbands in I Peter 3:7. What was Jesus' example described in I Peter 2?

Personal Holiness, Even When Persecuted
"Who did no sin, neither was guile found in his mouth: who, when he was reviled, reviled not again; when he suffered, he threatened not; but committed himself to him that judgeth righteously" (I Peter 2:22-23).

Total Commitment to the Father
"Who, when he was reviled, reviled not again; when he suffered, he threatened not; but committed himself to him that judgeth righteously" (I Peter 2:23).

Righteous Living
"Who his own self bare our sins in his own body on the tree, that we, being dead to sins, should live unto righteousness: by whose stripes ye were healed" (I Peter 2:24).

Shelter of Refuge in Himself
"For ye were as sheep going astray; but are now returned unto the Shepherd and Bishop of your souls" (I Peter 2:25).

I Peter 3:1 says *"likewise ye wives,"* pointing every mother back to the principles of Christ mentioned above. You may be asking, "How can I attain these lofty goals?" No one will get there without the aid of the Holy Spirit and the instruction of Scripture. But I Peter 3 lists some areas whereby a mother may exhibit the character of Christ:

🌴 A Chaste Conversation 🌴

"While they behold your chaste conversation coupled with fear" (I Peter 3:2).

The word *conversation* means behavior. *Chaste* has several meanings: proper, clean, innocent, modest, or perfect. Coupled together, the gist of *chaste conversation* is "a proper and pure lifestyle." Every Christian mother ought to be living just such a life. In context, Peter says that is the way that unbelievers are really won to Christ.

What is the driving factor that produces such a clean and pure lifestyle? Such behavior only comes when there is a Godly fear in our lives. *"While they behold your chaste conversation coupled with fear"* (I Peter 3:2). It is as we keep Him in perspective as our Father, Friend, Ruler, and Final Judge that such a lifestyle is lived.

🌴 A Whole Heart 🌴

"But let it be the hidden man of the heart, in that which is not corruptible, even the ornament of a meek and quiet spirit, which is in the sight of God of great price" (I Peter 3:4).

🌴 A New Heart 🌴

The heart, as used here, is the innermost part of us, the soul and spirit. That part of us, although unseen, is the ruler of our actions. In Matthew 12:34-35, Jesus explains, *"For out of the abundance of the heart the mouth speaketh. A good man out of the good treasure of the heart bringeth forth good things: and an evil man out to the evil treasure bringeth forth evil things."*

Jesus said in Matthew 15:18-20, *"But those things which proceed out of the mouth come forth from the heart; and they defile the man. For out of the heart proceed evil thoughts, murders, adulteries, fornications, thefts, false witness, blasphemies: These are the things which defile a man: but to eat with unwashen hands defileth not a man."* He says that it is from the heart that people are defiled. He said of the Pharisees, *"Their heart is far from me."* Before there can be any lifestyle of Christ, there must be a new heart. Salvation is the process of regeneration of the heart. Mothers must be born again to receive a new heart!

🌴 An Adorned Heart 🌴

A new heart does not entirely equip us for a separated lifestyle, as most of you will readily assent. There must be a continual work going on in our hearts. *"For which cause we faint not; but though our outward man perish, yet the inward man is renewed day by day"* (II Corinthians 4:16). Peter describes this renewing as *"the adorning of the hidden man of the heart."* To adorn is to put into an orderly arrangement, to decorate.

Saved people begin with a new heart that is entirely the work of God. Placing our heart in order is our work; we call it spiritual growth. Mother, you need time alone with the Lord every day. You need to pray every day. You need to read your Bible every day. As you give yourself to these, you will find you are adorning a heart that yearns to be more like Christ.

🌴 A Submissive Spirit 🌴

"But let it be the hidden man of the heart, in that which is not corruptible, even the ornament of a meek

and quiet spirit, which is in the sight of God of great price" (I Peter 3:4).

Meek—The word meek means humble. It is as we adorn our hearts with the Word of God and seek the presence of God that our inner man is tenderized. It may not be our nature to be submissive, but it is not through our nature that we serve the Lord. We will have no trouble with humbleness if we keep God in perspective. The mighty warrior, King David, cried *"Who am I?"* when faced with God's presence. *"The sacrifices of God are a broken spirit"* (Psalms 51:17).

Quiet—The second trait of a submissive heart is tranquility in spirit. It is only as we give ourselves, our problems, our very lives to the Lord that we come to this place of peace. *"Great peace have they which love thy law: and nothing shall offend them"* (Psalm 119:165). It is in the adornment of our heart that the peace comes. Mother, as you place your life in order before the Lord, expect peace. As you adorn your heart with the fear of the Lord, the Word of God, and prayer, the natural result will be peace and humbleness. It is not worked out, it is produced in the presence of the Lord.

Mother, *"Be in subjection to your own husbands"* (I Peter 3:1), may seem to be unattainable to you. You may say, "I can't submit to my husband. I will never be able to win him to the Lord." If you are saved, turn yourself over to Him. Let Him adorn your heart. You will be amazed at the results. The Bible says in the sight of God the meek and quiet spirit is of great price (I Peter 3:4).

*A virtuous woman is a crown to her husband.
Her children arise up, and call her blessed;
her husband also, and he praiseth her.*
Proverbs 12:4; 31:28

The Dana Dice family, home missionaries to New York City.

22

A Place of Mother's Love for Her Husband

The role of a mother is one of great responsibility. The Christian father has the responsibility of setting standards and providing the leadership in these. However, most of the time it is the mother whose abilities establish these standards in practice in the home. As stated earlier, she is the super-glue that holds everything together and the lubricant by which it all runs smoothly.

There are many tools that are required to be a successful Christian mother. As the title suggests, the overriding quality that must be present is love. I Peter 3:1-4, our scriptures used in the last chapter, teach us that in every area the mother (as every Christian) must follow the example of Christ. There are four areas where love is the dominant theme. In this chapter we will focus on Mother's love for her husband. Mother, remember that in this area, as well as all others, you set the example that will be followed by your children.

How should you love your husband? This is a question that needs to be answered for experienced wives and mothers as well as newlyweds and prospective moms.

🌲 Love Him Foremost, Surpassing All Others 🌲

When asked about divorce, Jesus answered, *"And said, For this cause shall a man leave father and mother, and shall cleave to his wife: and they twain shall be one flesh? Wherefore they are no more twain, but one flesh. What therefore God hath joined together, let not man put asunder"* (Matthew 19:5-6). The relationship is committed to the Lord for unification. This is said of no other relationship on earth. All others in your life become secondary to this relationship. *"Leave father and mother...cleave...become one."* You must love him enough to put him before housework, job, children, friends, etc. All other relationships in the home, even in your life, depend upon the success of this love relationship.

🌴 Love Him Practically 🌴

"The heart of her husband doth safely trust in her, so that he shall have no need of spoil. She will do him good and not evil all the days of her life...She riseth also while it is yet night, and giveth meat to her household, and a portion to her maidens...She is not afraid of the snow for her household: for all her household are clothed with scarlet" (Proverbs 31:11, 15, 21).

Hollywood paints an idealistic picture of lust and sentimentality and calls it love. But love is shown in the day by day. Love is practical—warm meals, a clean house, bearing and rearing children, and the keeping of his clothing. Because we live in the day of working wives and "liberated women," you may say that this is old-fashioned advice. No, it is Bible.

🌴 Love Him to Kingship 🌴

The Bible says that God made man in his own image and gave him the dominion in the earth. *"And God said, Let us make man in our image, after our likeness: and let them have dominion over the fish of the sea, and over the fowl of the air, and over the cattle, and over all the earth, and over every creeping thing that creepeth upon the earth"* (Genesis 1:26). The man that God created was the king! Genesis 2:18 says that God saw his need of a help meet. God gave the king a queen in his loneliness.

Wife, your husband is your origin, head, protector, and provider. Wonderful things happen when you honor the man in your life, if for nothing else than the position that God has given him.

Contrary to the dogma of the present day women's movement, Mother, when you love your husband as God intended, you don't become less in your station of life. The Bible says you become great! *"A virtuous woman is a crown to her husband"* (Proverbs 12:4). The promise of Scripture is the honor of children and the public praise of your husband. *"Her children arise up, and call her blessed; her husband also, and he praiseth her"* (Proverbs 31:28).

🌲 Love Him in Kindness 🌲

The old saying is that you can catch more flies with honey than you can with vinegar. Mother, the book of Proverbs reiterates this theme when it comes to your relationship with your husband. It is said of the virtuous woman in Proverbs 31:26, *"She openeth her mouth with wisdom; and in her tongue is the law of kindness."* The emphasis here is upon the tongue. Her words are well thought out. When she speaks, it is in words of kindness.

This verse is in contrast to Proverbs 21:19, *"It is better to dwell in the wilderness, than with a contentious and an angry woman." "It is better to dwell in the corner of the housetop, than with a brawling woman and in a wide house"* (Proverbs 25:24). *"A continual dropping in a very rainy day and a contentious woman are alike"* (Proverbs 27:15). When God has so much to say about a subject, we do well to pay heed.

🌲 Love Him with Consideration 🌲

Selfishness is the driving force behind most of the troubles in a marriage. One of the big areas of concern is finances. I know that some homes are in financial chaos because of the selfish spending of the husband. But this lesson is written to mothers. Mother, shopping should not become your means of recreation. The shopping mall is a place where the merchants tempt you to spend your money. Avoid that temptation. *"Watch and pray, that ye enter not into temptation: the spirit indeed is willing, but the flesh is weak"* (Matthew 26:41).

Again, Proverbs gives an example of the virtuous woman. *"She considereth a field, and buyeth it: with the fruit of her hands she planteth a vineyard"* (Proverbs 31:16). She has used her money wisely, not to squander away the provision of the house. Instead she has increased, or at least attempted to increase, the material blessings of the home.

Mother, you may be in a bad marriage situation. You may be saying, "But I don't love my husband." May I remind you that the vow you took was a holy vow. God never said, "Love your husband unless someone better comes along," "Love your husband unless you are incompatible," "Love your husband unless you are smarter," "Love your husband unless you make more money." No, He said, forsaking all others. *"They are no more twain, but one flesh. What therefore God hath joined together, let not man put asunder"* (Mark 10:8,9).

Love is energy expended toward another with no hope of anything in return. But as you give love, love is returned. I challenge you, Mother, to test the principles of the Bible. Put forth the energy to love your husband. You may be surprised at the results.

2 3

A Place of Mother's Love
Her Children

The Bible foresees the day in which we live. Two young mothers have been convicted recently for the murder of their beautiful young children. Everyday children are abandoned, mistreated, or without the love of a mother. Why is this? Paul describes these days as *"perilous times"* in II Timothy 3. He describes them as days of *"unnatural affection."* There is nothing more unnatural than the lack of a mother's love for her children. As a mother, God has certainly given you a natural affection for your children. It behooves you to prayerfully and scripturally allow that natural affection to become the Biblical love that the Lord intended.

🌲 Recognize Your Heritage 🌲

"Lo, children are an heritage of the LORD: and the fruit of the womb is his reward" (Psalm 127:3). Eve recognized this great truth. When Cain was born, she said, *"I have gotten a man, from the Lord"* (Genesis 4:2). Much could be said about this verse. For our purpose, notice that the man was gotten from the Lord. Mother, your children should not be looked upon as a burden or a hindrance to keep you from being free to do what you want. This is a lie that is sold to our society today. No, children are a

heritage of the Lord—they are God's gift to you. He has entrusted you with the great privilege of raising those children for Him. No person on earth has ever been entrusted with a greater calling and responsibility.

From the day of conception, your influence is the single greatest influence your child will ever know. By the time the child is three years old, his basic character traits have been shaped for the rest of his life. Others will have some part of shaping these character traits, but God has allowed you to be primary in the process. No other single individual on earth has this much power of influence over another. It is your heritage that God allows you to be a mother. Far from being a burden or hindrance, your children give you a place of great value in God's eyes.

🌲 Love Them to Hope 🌲

"But thou art he that took me out of the womb: thou didst make me hope when I was upon my mother's breasts" (Psalm 22:9). The only place of hope is in the Lord. From the time your children are nursing babies, you need to instill in them the hope that is ours in Him.

Instruct Them

The best place for Christian education of children is at the feet and in the lap of a Christian mother. You teach them with your lifestyle as well as with your words. Teaching is to be both by precept and practice. The children of Israel were instructed to teach their children in just this manner in Deuteronomy 6:6-9, *"And these words, which I command thee this day, shall be in thine heart: And thou shalt teach them diligently unto thy children, and shalt talk of them when thou sittest in thine house, and when thou walkest by the way, and when thou liest down, and when thou risest up. And thou shalt bind them for a sign upon thine hand, and they shall be as frontlets between thine eyes. And thou shalt write them upon the posts of thy house, and on thy gates."* Christianity should not be a Sunday thing. Your children should see it in you as an everyday thing.

Pray for Them

Don't forget to pray for your children. Hannah is an example of a praying mother. *"For this child I prayed"* (I Samuel 1:27-28). John Wesley and Charles Wesley became great men of God. John became one of the greatest preachers of the eighteenth century, and Charles' hymns are still sung today. Their testimony of Christian service began with a praying mother.

Listen to Them

Take time for your children. Converse with them about the things that are important to them. Take time to listen to problems they have. It may seem a small thing to you, but it is earth-shaking to them. Open communication is one of the keys to keeping their heart.

Correct Them

The Bible makes this area of correction very clear. *"He that spareth his rod hateth his son: but he that loveth him chasteneth him betimes"* (Proverbs 13:24). There are all kinds of excuses for failure to discipline. It will take character on your part to be the disciplinarian that the Lord wants you to be. Dr. James Dobson wrote a book entitled *Dare To Discipline.* If you will dare, your children will love you for it.

🌴 Love Them Practically 🌴

Keep them clean. Make your home a place of cheer, warmth, and hospitality. Make sure to welcome their friends to your home. Take time to cook good, warm meals for them. Give them yourself. A daughter writes,

"Then there was the priceless gift of your presence. I recall the fall afternoons when I rushed home from school to a kitchen steaming with the aroma of bubbling tomato juice or the spicy-sweet smell of vats of pickles.

Sometimes when we burst through the door, we heard the hum of the sewing machine. Even the cheery, whistling teakettle was a welcome sound—we knew you were home....There were probably times when you might have wished to work outside our home. But the gift of your presence meant more to me than anything we might have gotten with those extra dollars."

🌲 Love Them Personally 🌲

Mother, remember that no one else can fill your shoes. If you will not be a Christian mother to your children, they will have no Christian mother. God has given them to you and you to them. Children may find surrogate mothers at the church, school, or friends, but no one can fill your role. You are irreplaceable to your children's development to Christian adulthood.

There is no daycare center or baby sitter that can do the things outlined above or the innumerable other things that God has chosen you to do for your children. Though others may love them and care for them, Mother, your children need you. In God's description of a Christian mother, He indicates that she is to be the supplier that others depend on to have needs met. *"She stretcheth out her hand to the poor: yea, she reacheth forth her hands to the needy"* (Proverbs 31:20).

Mother, take the challenge. Be all that the Lord has chosen you to be. Be a real Christian mother. Realize the place of honor that you hold. Yes, the responsibilities are great, but the rewards are eternal. *"Her children arise up, and call her blessed; her husband also, and he praiseth her"* (Proverbs 31:28).

24

A Place of Mother's Love for Her Character

There are many aspects that complete the picture of the responsibility of the mother in the Christian home. As the title suggests, the overriding factor that must be present is love. Our aim is to investigate this love factor in the role of a Christian mother from a practical and logical perspective as we take the Bible as our instruction book.

We are following Paul's outline in Titus 2:4-5: *"That they may teach the young women to be sober, to love their husbands, to love their children, To be discreet, chaste, keepers at home, good, obedient to their own husbands, that the word of God be not blasphemed."* In past chapters we have noted, based on I Peter 3:1-4, the importance of a woman following Christ's example, loving her husband, and loving her children. She also must have a love (concern) for her own character.

The Hebrew writer describes the marriage relationship as *"honourable in all, and the bed undefiled"* (Hebrews 13:4). That is the Bible's view of the marriage relationship. It should be the desire of every Christian man or woman to meet and maintain this standard also. No Christian would knowingly go against the admonition of the Word of God. We are writing to Christian mothers, so we will look at the Scriptures from their point of view. Paul said, *"That they may teach the young women"* (Titus 2:4).

🌲 Learn Discretion—Knowledge 🌲

"To give subtilty to the simple, to the young man knowledge and discretion" (Proverbs 1:4). "As a jewel of gold in a swine's snout, so is a fair woman which is without discretion" (Proverbs 11:22). Webster's definition for discretion is "prudence, or knowledge, that enables a person to judge critically of what is correct and proper." In our everyday language we would probably say self-control.

God has put the standards for every area of life in the Scriptures. The application of the standard to our own lives is up to us. Mother, take the admonition of the Bible. Allow the wisdom of Bible principles to develop discretion in you. It can only happen as the mind of Christ becomes your mind and God's acceptable and perfect will becomes your will.

🌲 Be Chaste in Conduct 🌲

"For I am jealous over you with godly jealousy: for I have espoused you to one husband, that I may present you as a chaste virgin to Christ" (II Corinthians 11:2). *"While they behold your chaste conversation coupled with fear"* (I Peter 3:2). The word chaste means "free from all sexual commerce, or obscenity." This applies not only to adultery. It also means to be free from any indication or hint of sexuality, free from flirtation. As a wife and mother, there should never be anything in your actions that would cause a question in this area. *"The heart of her husband doth safely trust in her"* (Proverbs 31:11).

🌲 Be Careful in Dress 🌲

"In like manner also, that women adorn themselves in modest apparel, with shamefacedness and sobriety;

*not with broided hair, or gold, or pearls, or costly array;
But (which becometh women professing godliness) with
good works"* (I Timothy 2:9-10). Every mother should be
aware of her dress. The first statement of discretionary
character and chaste conduct any woman makes is with
her dress. There are some clear instructions given in the
Bible in this regard.

Modest Apparel

A Christian mother's dress should never draw
attention to her body. This will rule out tight slacks,
mini-skirts, low-cut blouses, and shorts (the Bible has
much to say about the baring of the thigh). Proverbs
describes a brazen woman who is dressed *"with the
attire of an harlot"* (Proverbs 7:10). We can readily
associate that attire in our minds as suggestive and
revealing, can't we? Most people let Hollywood or the
television networks dictate their dress. The media has
proven to be an advocate of the perverted and the
profane. We should allow the Word of God to instruct in
this area.

Suggestive Dress

Jesus said that a man who *"looketh on a woman to
lust after her hath committed adultery with her already
in his heart"* (Matthew 5:28). He said in Mark 7:21 that
adultery and fornication come *"from the heart of men."*
You cannot control the thoughts and lusts of another
heart. But Mother, your dress should never be such that
it incites these things in the heart of men. Avoid igniting
the flame of lust in a heart.

Feminine Dress

*"The woman shall not wear that which pertaineth
unto a man, neither shall a man put on a woman's
garment: for all that do so are abomination unto the
LORD thy God"* (Deuteronomy 22:5). There is a definite
difference between the sexes. God says we should make
the most of it. Mother, you will never be more beautiful

than when you dress and conduct yourself as the feminine person that you are. Don't let the pressure of this world dictate your dress. Dress in accord with God's instruction in this area. You may be surprised at the results.

Mother, I am aware that these are sensitive areas. It is with much prayer that I bring them before you. Some will say that it is not in the job description of a pastor to discuss them. Last year the school board in my area adopted a dress code for the school district in order to:

"Teach good grooming and hygiene, instill discipline and modesty, demonstrate respect for authority, prevent disruption, avoid safety hazards, and provide a successful learning environment. Appropriate dress and grooming standards promote responsibility and self esteem, thus fostering a sense of community for all students in their present and future interactions."[1]

If a secular organization can recognize these things and take the responsibility for doing something about them, shouldn't we, the Body of Christ, deal with them?

1 Dress Codes, Alvin Independent School District, Alvin, Texas.

25

A Place of Mother's Love for Her Home

"That they may teach the young women to be sober, to love their husbands, to love their children, to be discreet, chaste, keepers at home, good, obedient to their own husbands, that the word of God be not blasphemed" (Titus 2:4-5).

Paul's description of the Christian mother includes *keepers at home*. It is built into every Christian mother to want to have a home. Little girls grow up playing with dolls and dreaming of being a mother. The desire for a home is strong in a woman's natural makeup. In fact, in some cases the desire for a home exceeds her desire for a man. The home is the place where she finds fulfillment.

There is much unnecessary frustration and unhappiness among mothers today. They have bought the propaganda of the world that says that a mother and homemaker is a second-class citizen when compared to the "career girl" or "professional woman." Mother, don't believe it. God has placed you in an honored place as the wife of your husband, the mother of your children, and the administrator of your home. If God holds your position in high regard, who can lower it? Do not let peer pressure from the modern day feminist movement lower your position from that of a Christian mother.

Dr. Harold M. Voth, MD says, "I am well aware that many women must take jobs because of economic need.

Inflation is profoundly destructive to family life. I am also aware that, after children are well launched in life, it makes good sense for a woman to resume working outside the home if she so desires. But listen to this alarming statistic: 59% of women with children up to teenage are working, and 44% of working women have preschool children. The absence of these women, particularly those with preschool children, will almost always have a negative impact of some degree on childhood development. Small babies need object constancy, that is, the continuous input of good mothering by one person. Some of the most severe damage to human development can be done to the human spirit when the child-mother bond is discontinuous or broken during the first three years of life. Volumes have been written about this. When children are small and the mother is away most of the day, the quality of life in the home changes dramatically; only her presence will fill the void. I wish I could adequately convey to you the enormous importance of good mothering and only mature women can supply it. Good mothering from birth on provides the psychological core upon which all subsequent development takes place. Mothering is probably the most important function on earth. This is a full-time and demanding task."

Of course there are circumstances that require that a mother become a career woman, working in the job market. If you are a single working mother, my heart goes out to you. Your task is great. Don't think that the Lord doesn't understand the circumstance that you are in. The Bible has several examples of godly women who kept their family together by themselves. I believe you will be specially rewarded for your efforts to make a living and raise your children without the aid of a Christian father.

Included in the description of the seductive woman of Proverbs is this: *"She is loud and stubborn; her feet abide not in her house"* (Proverbs 7:11). To build a home, a Christian mother is a *keeper at home*. There are some distinguishing marks of the home that is filled with the love of a Christian mother.

A Place of Housekeeping

"And withal they learn to be idle, wandering about from house to house; and not only idle, but tattlers also and busybodies, speaking things which they ought not. I will therefore that the younger women marry, bear children, guide the house, give none occasion to the adversary to speak reproachfully" (I Timothy 5:13). Paul is not speaking of a spotless house but a kept house. He even gives guidelines: don't be idle, don't wander from house to house, don't be a busybody, and guard your tongue. Your responsibility is at home and is very great.

A Place of Goodness Shown

"Well reported of for good works; if she have brought up children, if she have lodged strangers, if she have washed the saints' feet, if she have relieved the afflicted, if she have diligently followed every good work" (I Timothy 5:10). It is a wonderful thing to be around a home where goodness is shown. All of us have warm memories of a mother like that. In addition to my own mother, I can recall aunts, grandmothers, and countless Christian mothers whose homes have been a warm place of refuge for the troubled or hurting, for neighbors, friends, and strangers alike. I watch young Christian mothers as they supply food, comfort, and advice for the various needs of the congregation here. Thank God for the goodness of Christian mothers.

A Place of Hospitality

"She stretcheth out her hand to the poor; yea, she reacheth forth her hands to the needy" (Proverbs 31:20). The Greek word that is translated hospitality means to be fond of guests. The Christian mother's home is open to those who will come. Hospitality is the mark of at

least two groups of people in the Bible. I Timothy 3:2 says the pastor is to be *"given to hospitality."* Taken from these two requirements, we can conclude that all Christians should show hospitality. Mother, your children and your husband should know that your home is open to those that they will bring into it.

Peter Marshall, the late preacher and chaplain of the Senate, said, "The world has enough women who know how to hold their cocktails, who have lost all their illusions and their faith. The world has enough women who know how to be smart. It needs women who are willing to be simple....Let us not fool ourselves— without Christianity, without Christian education, without the principles of Christ inculcated into young life, we are simply raising pagans.

"It remained for the twentieth century, in the name of progress, in the name of tolerance, in the name of broadmindedness, in the name of freedom, to pull [the Christian mother] down from her throne and try to make her like a man.

"She wanted equality. For nineteen hundred years she had not been equal—she had been superior. She wanted equality, and in order to obtain it she had to step down."

Mother, please don't step down. Love your home, love your husband, love your children, and love your character. You will never regret it. Your family will love you and God will honor you for it.

🌴 An Old-Fashioned Mother 🌴

She was just an old-fashioned mother,
She did not pretend to be "smart,"
To care for her home and her dear ones
Was the wish that was first in her heart.

We were raised by the old-fashioned methods,
So sparsely employed by today,
And when we so richly deserved it,
We were "spanked" in an old-fashioned way.

She taught us the old-fashioned virtue,
"A good name is far better," she'd say,
"Than all the wealth of the nation.
And truth is the best any day."

She believed in an old-fashioned Bible,
She trusted in old-fashioned prayer;
She told us that Jesus would hear us
If we'd speak anytime, anywhere.

She sits all alone most of the time now,
She rocks in an old rocking chair,
No longer a wife, no longer the teacher,
She's worn and wrinkled with old-fashioned care.

Some days, she's not really all here,
Her eye looks beyond, to a land all fair and all light,
Where Jesus and loved ones await her coming,
And an old-fashioned mother's faith will become sight.

By Wayne Hudson,
In honor of Mother, Beatrice Hudson
May 5, 1998

As arrows are in the hand of a mighty man; so are children of the youth. Happy is the man that hath his quiver full of them: they shall not be ashamed, but they shall speak with the enemies in the gate.
Psalm 127:4,5

After having two children of their own, Evangelist and Mrs. Ernie Perham adopted ten special-needs children (nine are pictured). The children often travel with their dad, and by their testimonies and songs they prove the effectiveness of Biblical principles for the family as Bro. Perham preaches family conferences in churches across the southeastern U.S.

26

A Place of Children

"Except the LORD build the house, they labour in vain that build it: except the LORD keep the city, the watchman waketh but in vain. It is vain for you to rise up early, to sit up late, to eat the bread of sorrows: for so he giveth his beloved sleep. Lo, children are an heritage of the LORD: and the fruit of the womb is his reward" (Psalm 127:1-3).

Children are to be a blessing to the home. But many today and through the years have been blighted treasures to many parents. Sometimes the parents are at fault, as Psalm 127:1-2 teaches. Their carnal desires for position and possession distract them from the responsibility of nurturing and bringing up children with Bible principles.

God says in Psalm 127:1-2 that the man in question here is not lazy. He is very aware of the need for a watchman to protect his material interests. He starts early and stays late. He knows the misery of sleepless nights. He is desperately trying to get ahead. He wants his children to have what he did not have as a child. The sad thing is this will never produce what God intended for the home to enjoy. God says it is of no profit. It would have been better to never have had the children than to only give them material things or to neglect to give them Jesus Christ.

Children can be seen in three categories:

🌴 Bringing Honor to the Lord in His House 🌴

"And Samuel grew, and the LORD was with him, and did let none of his words fall to the ground. And all Israel from Dan even to Beersheba knew that Samuel was established to be a prophet of the Lord" (I Samuel 3:19-20).

What a blessing it must have been to Hannah to see her son serving God in the temple of God. Her blessings could not be greater than those of a Christian mother or father today with children serving the Lord in His house, just taking their place among the many who serve Him with gladness.

Christian parents should pray first that their children should come to a saving knowledge of Christ early in life and then continue on to serve Him faithfully in the church. All other things necessary in life will be added to them if they will do this, according to Jesus Christ. *"But seek ye first the kingdom of God, and his righteousness; and all these things shall be added unto you"* (Matthew 6:33).

It is sad to see so many young people drift away from church after attending Sunday School and worship services all their lives. One of the most requested prayers of parents is for wayward children. Parent, this ought not to be. I beseech you to give the Lord a chance to build your house.

🌴 Blessing the Home of Their Parents 🌴

One of the great examples of Scripture is that of Joseph and his love and care of his father found in Genesis 37-50. As I read these chapters, I feel a great sense of peace because of this man who was such a blessing to his dad. As I visit in Christian homes, I have noticed that this same peace is there when children are saved and obedient to their parents. In other homes you can feel the tension. The parents are not sure what the children will say or do in your presence.

From the many words of Jacob concerning his son Joseph, from the many verses concerning Joseph's love for his dad, we can see that this son was a great blessing to his dad. The other sons brought misery to this man for many years of his life. Joseph, the son born of old age, seemed to bring joy to the heart of the father all his life. I noticed that he was a boy and a man of high character as he responded to wicked brothers, Potiphar, and Pharaoh, as well as with his dad. God truly had done a building work in this son of his father.

🌴 Breaking the Heart of Loving Parents 🌴

"And the king was much moved, and went up to the chamber over the gate, and wept: and as he went, thus he said, O my son Absalom, my son, my son Absalom! Would God I had died for thee, O Absalom, my son, my son!" (II Samuel 18:33).

One of the saddest pictures in the Bible is that of David in II Samuel 15:30, *"And David went up by the ascent of mount Olivet, and wept as he went up, and had his head covered, and he went barefoot: and all the people that was with him covered every man his head, and they went up, weeping as they went up."* The covered head and bare feet are both signs of shame for these Israelites. It was not a king who ascended mount Olivet, it was a broken-hearted parent. He was weeping for the sins of a willful son. True, David may have fault in this matter also. But that doesn't relieve the heartbreak.

Have ever sadder words been uttered than the words of weeping David? David, king of Israel, a man after the heart of God, a conqueror of man and beast, yet he saw his son Absalom destroyed by sin. How often does a pastor hear cries with this likeness, *"O my son Absalom, my son, my son Absalom! would God I had died for thee, O Absalom, my son, my son!"* (II Samuel 18:33).

How the heart of Adam and Eve must have suffered pain to see Cain driven away! How the heart of Samuel ached when none of his sons followed God! Many are the Christian homes this moment where sons and daughters are in sin and serving the world, the flesh, and the devil, while the hearts of moms and dads are breaking.

Children can be a treasure to the home. God wants to establish this treasure in the home. Christian parents want this treasure more than silver or gold. Parent or Grandparent, let the Lord build the house. Don't let the lusts and vanity of the world waste this most precious treasure. This is a treasure that will never tarnish, but will bring forth dividends, even in eternity. "The fruit of the womb is His reward."

27

The Legacy of the Home

Every home imparts a legacy to its children—whether Christian or otherwise. There are no exceptions. The question is, what kind of legacy?

🌴 Two Homes, Two Legacies 🌴

A few years ago a team of sociologists in New York state attempted to calculate the influence of a home environment on its children and the following generations. They researched the homes of two men who lived at the same time in the 18th century. One was Max Jukes, the other was Jonathan Edwards. The legacy of these two homes is a study in contrasts.

Max Jukes and his wife were unbelievers. He was a man of no principles. What was the legacy of their home? Among the 1,200 known descendants of Max Jukes were:

- 440 lives of outright debauchery
- 310 paupers and vagrants
- 190 public prostitutes
- 130 convicted criminals
- 100 alcoholics
- 60 habitual thieves
- 55 victims of impurity
- 7 murderers

Research showed that not one of Juke's descendants had made a significant contribution to society—not one! This notorious family had cost the state of New York $1,200,000. Not much of a legacy, is it?

What about the family of Jonathan Edwards? He was a noted pastor and an astute theologian. This renowned Christian was the instrument of God used to bring about the Great Awakening in colonial America. Later he served as the President of Princeton College. Jonathan Edwards came from a godly heritage and married Sarah, a woman of great faith. Together they built a home that left an entirely different legacy. Among their male descendants were:

- 300 clergy, missionaries, or theological professors
- 120 college professors
- 110 lawyers
- Over 60 physicians
- Over 60 authors of good books
- 30 judges
- 14 university presidents
- Numerous leaders in American industry
- 3 United States Congressmen
- 1 Vice President of the United States

Such is the lasting influence of one godly home. Now that's a legacy!

Every home leaves a legacy that will affect future generations for centuries to come. But let's face it, not all legacies are the same. Some are productive and illustrious. Others are destructive and infamous. How you build your home will affect generations to come. Again the question is, what kind of legacy will you leave behind?

🌲 What is a Legacy? 🌲

What comes to your mind when you hear the word legacy? Most often we think of a financial inheritance that is passed from one generation to the next. The Bible teaches that leaving a monetary legacy for one's children is honorable and commendable.

"A good man leaveth an inheritance to his children's children: and the wealth of the sinner is laid up for the just" (Proverbs 13:22).

"House and riches are the inheritance of fathers" (Proverbs 19:14).

As desirable as a financial legacy is, there are limitations and dangers in leaving behind the possessions of this world for our children. Many young people have been ruined by the sudden acquisition of wealth because they did not possess the maturity or the character to handle it. In addition, a financial legacy does not last. Nor can it bring true happiness. Jesus said life does not consist in the things that we have.

No, our homes need to leave behind a different kind of legacy. One that money cannot buy and taxes cannot take away. One that is intangible, invisible, and eternal. One that is far more valuable than silver or gold. I am talking about a spiritual legacy, one that will truly enrich our children's lives, mold their character, and impact their destiny. A Godly legacy is the only legacy really worth leaving.

Let's face it, far more important than leaving a financial estate is the bequeathing of a spiritual inheritance. Long after whatever personal investments you may leave your children are spent, a spiritual legacy will continue to compound daily and pay rich dividends for all eternity. Whatever the size of your financial inheritance may be, if that is all you leave your children, you leave them poor. But if your home is a place that imparts a spiritual legacy, you leave them rich. The Bible says in Proverbs 20:7, "The just man walketh in his integrity: his children are blessed (made rich) after him."

🌴 The Importance of your Legacy 🌴

The Christian home is the most important undertaking of your life. It was the first institution ordained by God.

It is the foundation of the church, human government, and our society. Its effect will be determined in the years and centuries to come. Its reward will be seen only in eternity. And, parent, it is completely in your hands.

No one else can build the Christian home for you, not the church, the preacher, your parents, psychologists, or society. God has placed your home in your hands. Please do not fail in your responsibility. Build it by the Book, on the principles of His Word. Give your children the legacy that will endure in their lives and in the generations that follow them. Give them your faith in Jesus Christ and the core values of His eternal kingdom.

It won't be easy to build a Christian home. At times it will be the greatest struggle you will ever face. One of the greatest battlegrounds in the spiritual warfare raging in the world today is the Christian home. You will have to work, sweat, cry, and maybe even be heartbroken. It will take a complete commitment to the Bible as it outlines the marriage relationships, the marriage responsibilities, and the principles for blessings in the Christian home that are *The Beams of Our House*.

The legacy of the Christian home is not automatically attained. It comes at great price. But the prize is worth the price. The legacy that you leave will be worth it all. It will be worth it here on earth and will be of untold value in eternity. An old commercial said, "Give the gift that keeps on giving". When you give the legacy of a Christian home, you give that gift that keeps on giving.

Bibliography

Barkman, Rev. Robert, *The Family.*

Buffington, J.B., *Mother's Apron Strings.*

Central Baptist Church, *The Baptist Challenge*, Little Rock.

Christenson, Larry, *The Christian Family.*

Dobson, Dr. James, *Focus On The Family Newsletter,* Colorado Springs, August 1994.

Farris, Michael, and Beverly Lahaye, *On This Day.*

Ironside, Harry A., *Notes On Proverbs*, Loizeaux Brothers, Neptune, N.J., 1975.

Jeremiah, Dr. David, *Home Improvement*, Turning Point, San Diego, 2001.

Marshall, Peter, "Keepers of the Springs", *Mr. Jones Meet the Master*, Revell, Grand Rapids, 1949.

Prater, Rev. Bill, *Heaven In the Home.*

Rice, Dr. John R., *The Home*, Sword of the Lord, Murfreesboro, 1946.

Rogers, Dr. Adrian, *Harmony In The Home*, message on tape.

Ward, Dr. Thomas, editor, *Family Time With God* and *Youth Time With God*, Partners In Ministry, Wilmington, DE.

Editor's Note
    What began as a series of articles for our church's bulletins grew to be a book as the Lord opened opportunities to use the material. It is possible that some references used in the original articles are no longer in our notes or library. We wish to apologize for any oversight that may become apparent and will acknowledge references in any future printings.